50 THINGS YOU SHOULD KNOW ABOUT INVENTIONS

by Clive Gifford

QED

Quarto is the authority on a wide range of topics.
Quarto educates, entertains and enriches the lives of
our readers—enthusiasts and lovers of hands-on living.
www.quartoknows.com

Design and Editorial: Tall Tree Ltd
Consultant: Dr Mike Goldsmith

Copyright © QED Publishing 2016

First published in the UK in 2016
by QED Publishing
Part of The Quarto Group
The Old Brewery, 6 Blundell Street
London, N7 9BH

A catalogue record for this book is
available from the British Library.

ISBN 978 1 78493 561 0

Printed in China

Words in **bold** are explained
in the glossary on page 78.

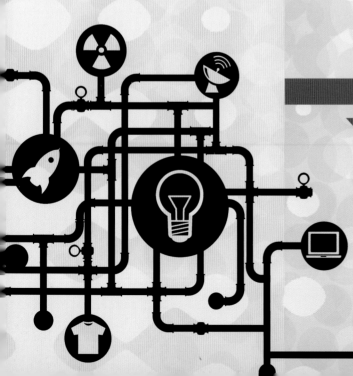

CONTENTS

		Page
	INTRODUCTION	4
1	**On the move**	6
2	**Bicycles**	8
3	**Hot-air balloons**	9
4	**Steam locomotives**	10
5	**Internal combustion engines**	11
6	**Motor cars**	12
7	**Early aircraft**	14
8	**Jet engines**	16
9	**Submarines**	18
10	**Rockets**	19
11	**Satellites**	20
12	**Manned spacecraft**	21
13	**Around the home**	22
14	**Central heating**	24
15	**Flushing toilets**	25
16	**Frozen food**	26
17	**Microwave ovens**	27
18	**Vacuum cleaners**	28

19	Ballpoint pens	29
20	Light bulbs	30
21	Fasteners	31
22	Communication	32
23	Printing press	34
24	Braille	35
25	Telegraph	36
26	Radio	37
27	Telephones	38
28	Computers	40
29	The Internet	42
30	World Wide Web	43
31	Inventions at work	44
32	Batteries	46
33	Dynamite	47
34	Electromagnets	48
35	Steam turbines	49
36	Plastics	50
37	Transistors	52
38	Lasers	53

39	Robots	54
40	Zooming in	56
41	Seeing inside the body	58
42	Lifesavers	60
43	That's entertainment	62
44	Moving pictures	64
45	Sound recording	66
46	Television	68
47	Trampolines	70
48	Snowboards	71
49	Video games	72
50	Inventing the future	74
	Who's who? Great inventors	76
	Glossary	78
	Index	80

INTRODUCTIO

Inventions are new **machines**, objects, materials or processes that did not exist before. Many inventions make people's lives easier, safer or more fun. Inventors often combine existing objects with scientific knowledge to create something **innovative** and exciting. Many inventions fail, but those that succeed can transform the way we live and work.

HARD WORK PAYS

Some inventions result from a sudden idea, but most require a lot of hard work. Inventors need patience and persistence to overcome obstacles and failures, to solve problems and to test and improve their inventions. British engineer James Dyson built 5,127 **prototypes** for his new type of bagless vacuum cleaner in the 1970s and 1980s before it was good enough to put on sale.

◀ *In addition to vacuum cleaners, Dyson has also invented numerous other products, including a type of wheelbarrow, a washing machine and a hand dryer.*

AHEAD OF THE GAME

Not all inventions are a roaring success straight away.

Tin opener: The first sealed tin can to store food was made in about 1810, but no one invented a tin opener until 40 years later! Early cans had to be opened with hammers and chisels.

Barcode: Bernard Silver and Joseph Woodland of the USA invented barcodes for identifying products between 1949 and 1952. However, the first barcode scanner that could read the codes and make the invention usable didn't appear in shops until 1974.

◀ *An early can opener, with handle, blade and hook.*

◀ *Lines of varying width create a unique product identity.*

▶ An 1890 portrait of Edison shows him testing his sound-recording phonograph in his famous laboratory at Menlo Park, New Jersey, USA.

THOMAS EDISON

Legendary US inventor Thomas Edison produced more than 1000 inventions during his long lifetime (1847–1931), including electric lamps (p30) and devices for recording sound (p66). He described inventing as, "one per cent inspiration and ninety-nine per cent perspiration."

OOPS!

Some inventions occur quite by chance (see Microwave oven, p27). Cornflakes were invented in 1894 when brothers John and Will Kellogg forgot about some cooked wheat that had gone stale. They tried to roll it into long strips of dough, only for small flakes to form. When baked, these flakes became the original version of the now world-famous breakfast cereal.

▼ Cornflakes, the product of chance discovery.

Computer mouse: Invented by US engineer Douglas Engelbart in 1963, the mouse was barely used until the mid-1980s when personal computers such as the Apple Macintosh 128 and the Atari ST adopted it.

▶ An early computer mouse, encased in polished wood.

On the move

People today may take transport for granted as they fly, sail or drive long distances. Years ago, however, such long journeys were impossible or, at best, difficult, time-consuming or dangerous. Many transport inventions have allowed people to explore all parts of the planet and beyond.

The first wheels were not used for transport but as potter's wheels.

► *A man rides a replica Roman chariot. The first chariots were invented in the Middle East about 4000 years ago.*

WHEEL AND AXLE

Wheels made of solid discs of wood were invented at least 5300 years ago, according to evidence found in central Europe, and Sumeria in modern-day Iraq. Before wheels, people dragged loads using ropes, or put rollers or skids underneath, which was slow and hard work. The later invention of a rod called an axle allowed wheels to spin freely and enabled large carts and wagons to be built. These could be pulled by horses or other animals to transport heavy loads far more easily than before.

Bicycles	**Hot-air balloons**	**Steam locomotives**	**Motor Cars**
The popular two-wheeled vehicle was invented in the early 19th century (see page 8).	These large envelopes filled with hot air enabled people to experience flight for the first time (see page 9).	The vehicles of the first motorized transport network were powered by steam (see page 10).	The internal combustion engine led to the creation of the motor car in 1885 (see pages 11–13).

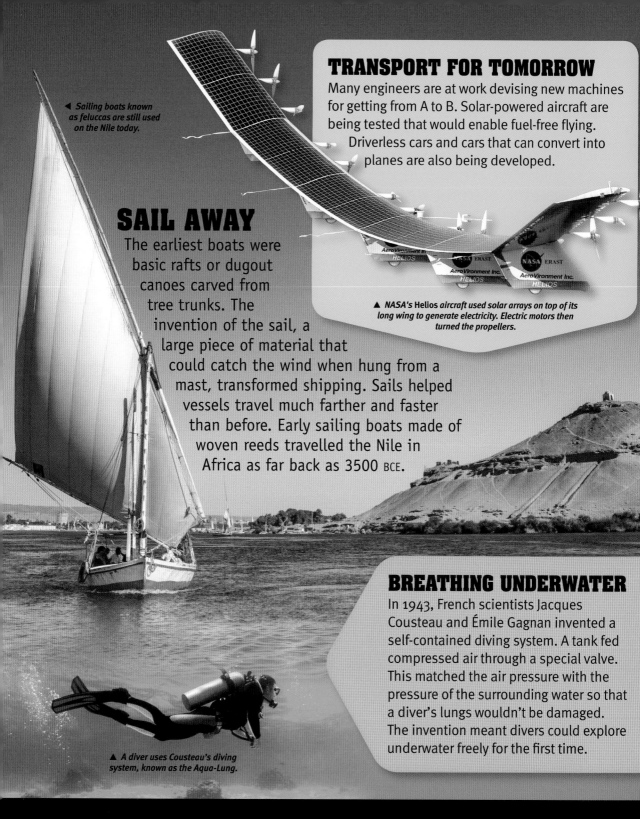

Sailing boats known as feluccas are still used on the Nile today.

TRANSPORT FOR TOMORROW

Many engineers are at work devising new machines for getting from A to B. Solar-powered aircraft are being tested that would enable fuel-free flying. Driverless cars and cars that can convert into planes are also being developed.

▲ NASA's Helios aircraft used solar arrays on top of its long wing to generate electricity. Electric motors then turned the propellers.

SAIL AWAY

The earliest boats were basic rafts or dugout canoes carved from tree trunks. The invention of the sail, a large piece of material that could catch the wind when hung from a mast, transformed shipping. Sails helped vessels travel much farther and faster than before. Early sailing boats made of woven reeds travelled the Nile in Africa as far back as 3500 BCE.

BREATHING UNDERWATER

In 1943, French scientists Jacques Cousteau and Émile Gagnan invented a self-contained diving system. A tank fed compressed air through a special valve. This matched the air pressure with the pressure of the surrounding water so that a diver's lungs wouldn't be damaged. The invention meant divers could explore underwater freely for the first time.

▲ A diver uses Cousteau's diving system, known as the Aqua-Lung.

Aircraft
The modern aviation industry began when the first powered flight took off in 1903 (see pages 14–15).

Jet engines
Modern airliners and many military aircraft rely on these powerful engines for their high speeds (see pages 16–17).

Submarines
People have been building vehicles that can travel underwater since the 17th century (see page 18).

Spacecraft
Satellites and manned space flights became possible with the invention of rockets (see pages 19–21).

Bicycles

The modern bicycle is the product of many inventors, starting with Baron Karl von Drais who built the 'Dandy Horse' in Germany in 1817. It had two wheels mounted on a frame that the rider moved by pushing the ground with their feet.

▲ Rod-powered two-wheeler

▼ A velocipede

▶ Riders pushed their feet along the ground to move the dandy horse forward.

◀ Penny farthings had a gigantic front wheel measuring up to 150 centimetres in diameter.

HIGH WHEELERS

Without gear systems, the only way to make faster versions of front-wheel pedal bikes was to fit larger wheels. Inventors such as Eugène Meyer in France and James Starley in England created 'penny farthing' bicycles in the 1870s. In 1884, British cyclist Thomas Stevens managed to ride a penny farthing across the United States – from San Francisco to Boston, a distance of nearly 5000 kilometres.

PEDAL POWER

In 1839, Scottish blacksmith Kirkpatrick Macmillan built a two-wheeler with pedals connected to the wheels by rods. Other inventors from the 1850s onwards fixed pedals to the axle of the front wheel, which were turned by the rider's feet. These fixed-pedal bikes were known as *velocipedes*, meaning 'fast foot' in French.

SAFETY BICYCLES

John Kemp Starley, a nephew of James Starley, invented his 'safety bicycle' in 1885. It featured a diamond-shaped frame, similar-sized wheels, and pedals below the rider that drove the rear wheel via a chain – all features found on bikes today.

◀ Modern mountain bikes have lightweight frames, 20 or more gears and suspension systems to cushion the bike and rider from dips and bumps.

Hot-air balloons

FIRST FLIGHT

A cockerel, a duck and a sheep were the first creatures to fly in a hot-air balloon, built by Joseph-Michel and Jacques-Étienne Montgolfier in Paris, France, in 1783. A few weeks later, the brothers' next balloon carried the first people – a soldier and a teacher – on a 23-minute flight that landed safely.

A hot-air balloon carries people in a basket slung beneath a giant bag called an envelope, which is filled with heated air. Early balloons used a small fire to heat the air, while modern balloons use a propane gas burner. The hot air is lighter than the colder air outside, causing the balloon to rise. A valve at the top releases hot air, allowing the balloon to descend.

▲ *Colourful balloons take to the air at a New Jersey balloon festival in 2015.*

GAS BALLOONS

Just ten days after the Montgolfiers' success, another passenger-carrying balloon took off in Paris. Built by Jacques Charles and the brothers Anne-Jean and Nicolas-Louis Robert, it was made of silk coated in rubber and inflated not with hot air but with hydrogen gas. This was much lighter than hot air and made the balloon fly higher than the Montgolfier balloon. However, hydrogen could (and often did) catch fire. Modern gas balloons are filled with the safer gas, helium.

During the US Civil War, hot-air balloons were used by both sides to spy on the enemy.

Steam locomotives

Most **steam engines** burn coal or wood to heat water in a boiler and make steam. The pressure of the steam pushes a rod called a **piston** inside a cylinder to produce mechanical power. It was English engineer Richard Trevithick who first built a steam engine that could propel a vehicle along rails.

▲ At Trevithick's 1808 'Steam Circus' in London, passengers could ride his Catch Me Who Can around a track.

PEN-Y-DARREN PIONEER

Trevithick's **locomotive** made its first journey in 1804, hauling five wagons, 70 people and 10 tonnes of iron from the ironworks at Pen-y-darren in Wales to the Merthyr-Cardiff Canal, 15.8 kilometres away. It reached a top speed of 8 kilometres per hour.

STEPHENSON'S LOCOMOTIVES

Others soon began building locomotives. The most famous is George Stephenson, whose *Locomotion No.1* and *Locomotion No.2* operated on the Stockton and Darlington Railway in England in 1825. This was the world's first public cargo and passenger rail service.

◀ Stephenson designed a new boiler that generated much more power. In 1829, it enabled his new locomotive, The Rocket, to reach speeds of 45 kilometres per hour.

▼ In 1938, the Mallard became the world's fastest steam locomotive, reaching 202.58 kilometres per hour.

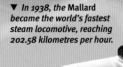

THE AGE OF STEAM

Steam locomotives began a revolution in transport, allowing fast travel over long distances for the first time. A railway boom occurred worldwide. In the United States, for example, there were just 63 kilometres of railway lines in 1830. By 1890, there were 261,770 kilometres.

Internal combustion engines

As an alternative to steam, several engineers built engines that burned gas or oil inside metal cylinders. These created expanding gases that drove a piston down. A shaft connected to the piston converted the up-and-down movement into a motion that could turn wheels.

OTTO'S ENGINE

Nikolaus Otto was a German engineer who came up with a four-stroke petrol **internal combustion engine** in 1876 (stroke refers to the number of movements made by a piston during each cycle, see below). It proved so reliable that more than 30,000 were built in the first 10 years.

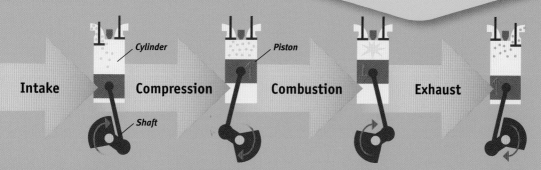

Intake — Cylinder — Piston

Compression — Shaft

Combustion

Exhaust

FOUR-STROKE CYCLE

Intake: Air and fuel (most commonly, petrol) enter an engine cylinder through an opening called a valve.
Compression: The piston rises up the cylinder, squeezing the fuel and air mixture together.

Combustion: A spark plug ignites the fuel and air. The expanding gases made by the burning mixture drives the piston down the cylinder.
Exhaust: As the piston rises, it pushes the waste gases out of the cylinder and into the **exhaust** system.

POPULAR POWER

The internal combustion engine proved a versatile way of producing power, allowing the development of motor vehicles, engine-driven lawnmowers and large power tools such as chainsaws. In the 1900s, US engineers Cameron Waterman and Ole Evinrude both invented outboard motors with an internal combustion engine.

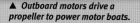

▲ *Outboard motors drive a propeller to power motor boats.*

Most modern car engines have more than one piston and cylinder to produce power.

At peak production, a completed *Model T* left Ford's assembly line every 10 seconds.

12

In 1769, French inventor Nicolas-Joseph Cugnot built a steam-powered vehicle. It had a top speed of just 3 kilometres per hour, but it was the world's first automobile. Other steam vehicles were built in the 1800s, but it took a petrol-fuelled engine to make motor cars practical and popular.

BENZ'S THREE WHEELER

German engineer Karl Benz produced the first petrol car, the *Benz Patent Motorwagen*, in 1885. This three-wheeler became the first car to go on sale in 1888. To promote the vehicle, Benz's wife, Bertha, used it to make the first long car journey – 189 kilometres from Mannheim to Pforzheim and back.

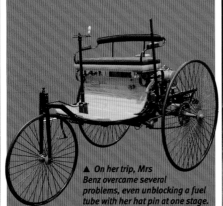

▲ On her trip, Mrs Benz overcame several problems, even unblocking a fuel tube with her hat pin at one stage.

PRODUCTION CARS

Benz's four-wheeled *Velo* of 1894 was the first car manufactured in large numbers, with 1200 built. By 1913, US industrialist Henry Ford revolutionized car making by using moving assembly lines where car bodies had their parts fitted. As a result, cars became faster and cheaper to make.

STAR CARS

MODEL T FORD

Built from 1908 to 1927, the *Model T* was the first **mass-produced** car, with more than 16 million built. By the mid-1920s, half of all the world's cars were this model.

VOLKSWAGEN *BEETLE*

Produced from 1938 to 2003, the much-loved *Beetle* became one of the world's best-selling cars, with more than 21.5 million sold.

RECORD BREAKERS

Longest car: 30 metres – Jay Ohrberg's American Dream limousine. It has 26 wheels and contains a swimming pool and a helicopter landing pad!

Smallest production car: At 137 centimetres long by 99 centimetres wide – the *Peel P50*. The car weighs 59 kilograms and has no reverse gear. Drivers have to pull the vehicle backwards.

Fastest production car: Top speed of 420 kph – the *Bugatti Chiron,* successor to the *Bugatti Veyron Super Sport*. The car can accelerate from 0–100 kilometres per hour in 2.5 seconds.

▲ *Airbag systems detect a very sudden drop in speed and fire gases to inflate a protective nylon bag.*

CAR SAFETY

Many inventions have made cars safer. In 1903, US inventor Mary Anderson made the first windscreen wipers, while 1949 saw the invention of the first crash test dummy. These lifelike models of humans are fitted with sensors to measure the effect of collision impacts on people.

▲ *The engine in a Bugatti Veyron has 16 cylinders.*

MONSTER TRUCKS

In 1979, Bob Chandler invented a monster pickup truck called *Bigfoot*, which had oversized tyres and suspension. Monster trucks now thrill crowds by racing and performing tricks in arenas.

TOYOTA *PRIUS*

The first production hybrid car, the *Prius* went on sale in 1997. Its electric wheel motors and a regular internal combustion engine resulted in better fuel economy and less pollution.

Early aircraft

The *Flyer 1* weighed just 274.4 kg – 2000 times lighter than a modern *Airbus A380-800*.

On 17 December 1903, at Kill Devil Hills in the US state of North Carolina, Orville Wright made the first powered, controlled flight in a heavier-than-air machine, the *Flyer 1*. Orville's flight may have only lasted 12 seconds and covered just 36 metres, which is shorter than many modern airliners, but it gave birth to the age of aviation.

FROM BIKES TO FLIGHTS

Orville and Wilbur Wright were brothers who ran a bicycle-making business in Dayton, Ohio, which they used to explore their fascination with machines. The Wright brothers applied their self-taught engineering skills to all aspects of aircraft design. They built kites and made more than 200 flights in their own gliders, and even constructed a homemade wind tunnel to test out their designs.

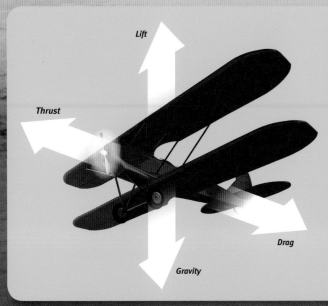

Lift

Thrust

Drag

Gravity

FOUR FORCES

Aircraft designers have to contend with four **forces**. An aircraft's wings have to generate enough lift to overcome the force of **gravity,** which pulls objects back towards the Earth. To move forwards, an aircraft's engine has to generate lots of **thrust** to overcome drag – the force of friction and air resistance which slows objects down as they move through air.

The Wrights learned that, once an aircraft was in the air, it could rotate in one of three ways known as roll, pitch and yaw. A successful plane has to control these directions of movement. The Wrights fitted their aircraft with rudders for yaw and elevators for pitch. They also invented an innovative system using wires to bend the wing tips so that the plane could roll while in flight.

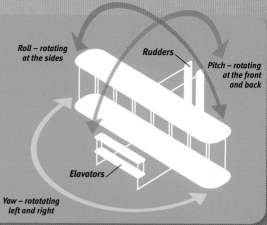

Roll – rotating at the sides

Rudders

Pitch – rotating at the front and back

Elavators

Yaw – rotatating left and right

◄ The Flyer 1, shown here during its first flight, had propellers mounted on its wings. Orville lay down to reduce drag. He also used wires attached to his hips to move the rudders and bend the wings.

BIPLANES AND MONOPLANES

The Wrights' achievements inspired aviation mania. In 1909, Frenchman Louis Blériot flew the English Channel between France and England. Unlike the Wrights' biplanes, his monoplane had just a single pair of wings and a single **propeller** mounted at the front – a design still used today in many aircraft.

▲ A modern replica of the Blériot XI, the plane in which Louis Blériot crossed the English Channel.

MOVING ON UP

Aircraft developed rapidly during the early 20th Century.

1919 The first non-stop flight across the Atlantic Ocean is made in a *Vickers Vimy* bomber.

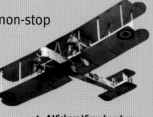

▲ A Vickers Vimy bomber, pictured during World War I.

1928 The first accurate barometric altimeter is invented by the German Paul Kollsman. This let pilots know what altitude (height above the ground) they were flying at.

1938 The first airliner with a pressurized cabin, the *Boeing 307*, enters service. It could fly far higher than rival planes allowing it to cruise above most weather disturbances.

1939 The first practical helicopter, the *Sikorsky VS-300*, makes its maiden flight. Helicopters use long rotor blades spun through the air to generate lift.

Jet engines

Until the 1940s, all aircraft were powered by a piston engine that spun a propeller. Jet engines generated much more thrust so aircraft could accelerate faster. They could also operate at much higher altitudes than propeller-driven planes.

INVENTOR V INVENTOR

In the 1920s and 1930s, two engineers, Hans von Ohain in Germany and Frank Whittle in England, worked independently on their own versions of the first jet engines. Whittle was the first to receive a **patent** in 1930 and bench-tested his prototype engine in April 1937, a few months before von Ohain's engine first ran. The German engineer, however, was the first to see his engine fly when it powered a *Heinkel He178* experimental aircraft in August 1939.

HOW JETS WORK

Jet engines take in air, mix it with fuel and burn it in combustion chambers. This produces large quantities of gases that expand out of the rear exhaust of the engine. Because these gases produce a backwards-travelling thrust, an equal and opposite reaction force occurs, propelling the aircraft forwards. This principle was first described by English mathematician Sir Isaac Newton in 1687 and is known as Newton's Third Law of Motion. It states that for every action, there is an equal and opposite reaction.

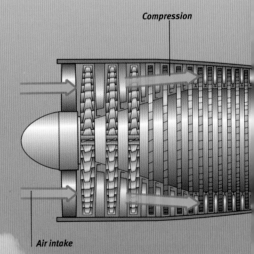

Compression

Air intake

JET STARS

1952
DE HAVILLAND COMET
The first commercial jet airliner entered service with BOAC. Four turbojet engines gave it a range of 2400 kilometres.

1976
LOCKHEED SR-71 BLACKBIRD
This spy plane became the fastest jet aircraft in level flight when it achieved a speed of 3529.6 kilometres per hour, flying over California, USA.

▼ The 7.48-metre-long Heinkel He178 reached a speed of 598 kilometres per hour on its trial flights. Air for its single jet engine entered through the plane's nose and then mixed with diesel fuel.

◄ Here, Whittle's jet engines power the Gloster E28/39 (also known as the Gloster Whittle) in its first flight in 1941.

VTOL

Some jet aircraft are able to alter the direction of their engine's thrust to vertically take off or land, an attribute known as VTOL. The first VTOL jet aircraft to enter military service was the *Hawker Siddeley Harrier* in 1969. Subsequent versions of the plane have been built to take off and land vertically from the decks of ships.

Air and fuel mixed and burned in combustor.

Exhaust

◄ A turbojet works by burning the air-fuel mixture in the combustor and blasting the hot, high-pressure air through a turbine and a nozzle.

▲ The Harrier was designed to operate from urban areas or forest clearings, without the need for an air base that would be vulnerable to attack.

Turbine

Nozzle

1988
ANTONOV AN-225
The An-225 is the heaviest plane ever. It has a maximum take-off weight of 640,000 kg. Its giant wings hold six jet engines.

2007
AIRBUS A-380
The world's largest jet airliner features a double deck passenger cabin and can hold up to 853 passengers.

2016
BOEING 777-200LR
Emirates airline began the world's longest non-stop scheduled flights – 14,200 km from Dubai to New Zealand.

Submarines

Submarines are underwater vehicles used by the military and armed with self-propelled weapons called torpedoes. One early idea for a submarine came from English innkeeper William Bourne, who in 1580 described how a craft that could change how much water it displaced (pushed away) could be made to rise or dive.

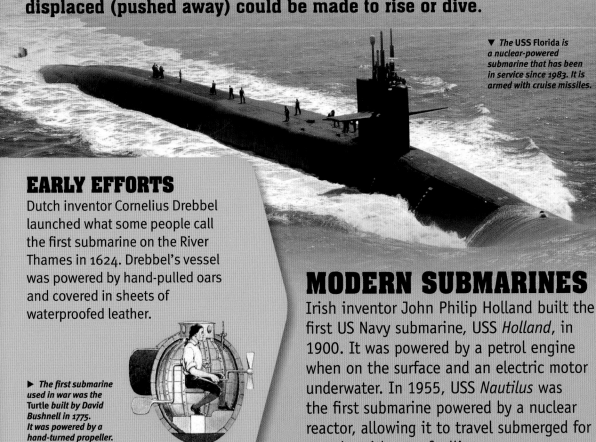

▼ *The* USS Florida *is a nuclear-powered submarine that has been in service since 1983. It is armed with cruise missiles.*

EARLY EFFORTS

Dutch inventor Cornelius Drebbel launched what some people call the first submarine on the River Thames in 1624. Drebbel's vessel was powered by hand-pulled oars and covered in sheets of waterproofed leather.

▶ *The first submarine used in war was the Turtle built by David Bushnell in 1775. It was powered by a hand-turned propeller.*

MODERN SUBMARINES

Irish inventor John Philip Holland built the first US Navy submarine, USS *Holland*, in 1900. It was powered by a petrol engine when on the surface and an electric motor underwater. In 1955, USS *Nautilus* was the first submarine powered by a nuclear reactor, allowing it to travel submerged for months without refuelling.

RISE AND FALL

A modern submarine can dive or rise by altering how much water is held in its giant ballast tanks. In most submarines, these are found between the outer shell and the interior.

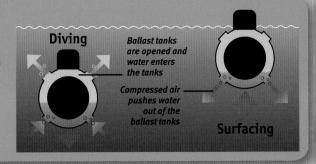

Diving

Ballast tanks are opened and water enters the tanks

Compressed air pushes water out of the ballast tanks

Surfacing

Underwater vehicles called submersibles have descended over 10,000 m to the ocean floor.

◀ The Space Shuttle used two boosters and its own rockets to blast into orbit.

Rockets

Inventors knew that to travel into space a huge amount of power was needed to escape Earth's gravity. The problem was that most types of engine needed to mix their fuel with oxygen from air and there is no air in space. The answer was to build rocket engines that could carry both fuel and oxygen.

◀ Goddard's first liquid-fuelled rocket was just 3 .4 metres tall and weighed 2.7 kilograms.

THRUST

Space rockets contain giant tanks of fuel and liquid oxygen (or an oxygen-providing substance called an oxidiser). These are pumped into a large combustion chamber. There, they are burned and create gases that expand and travel very quickly out of the nozzle at the base of the rocket. Speeds of over 3700 metres per second have been measured! The gases create huge amounts of thrust that power the rocket up and away.

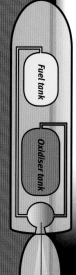

Fuel tank

Oxidiser tank

Combustion chamber

FROM MISSILES TO MISSIONS

Small gunpowder rockets were invented in China more than 800 years ago. Not until 1926 did US engineer Robert Goddard launch the world's first liquid-fuelled rocket. It flew for only 2½ seconds, but it was a major step forward. In Germany, Wernher von Braun invented the *V-2* during World War II, the first long-range rocket-powered missile. After the war, Sergei Korolev masterminded the Soviet Union's rocket missile program. Versions of his R-7 rockets, called *Vostok*, sent the first satellite and first astronaut into space.

▲ The V-2 rocket could reach an altitude of 88 kilometres before diving towards its target.

Satellites

Artificial satellites are man-made objects that orbit the Earth. The very first, *Sputnik 1*, was developed by the Soviet Union's space programme. It was launched into space by a rocket adapted from a type of long-distance missile in 1957.

SPACE AIDS

More than 6000 satellites have been launched since *Sputnik 1*, performing a great variety of tasks. Some relay television, telephone or Internet signals between different parts of the planet, while others help track storms and map wind and cloud formations from above to aid weather forecasting.

▼ *The* Landsat 8 *is an Earth observation satellite launched in 2013. It monitors seasonal changes on Earth's surface.*

BEEP TEST

Sputnik 1 was a metal sphere 58.5 centimetres in diameter. It had three batteries, a temperature control mechanism, a thermometer, a pressure measuring device and a radio transmitter that sent back a series of beeps via *Sputnik's* four antennae. These signals were heard by radio receivers all over the world for 21 days before its batteries ran out.

SAT NAV

▼ *Signals received by a car sat nav can be used to plot a route.*

A network of more than 20 satellites provides accurate navigation on Earth for anyone using a global positioning system (GPS). The satellites transmit signals to the GPS receiver. The receiver then measures tiny differences in time between the signals from each satellite to calculate a precise location on Earth.

In 2009, a US and a Russian satellite were destroyed when they collided in space.

Manned spacecraft

In 1961, a Soviet cosmonaut named Yuri Gagarin became the first human in space aboard the *Vostok 1* spacecraft. Gagarin sat inside a 2.3-metre-wide ball of steel covered in a heat shield to protect him as the craft re-entered the atmosphere. Three portholes gave him views of Earth and space never seen before.

▲ *Gagarin orbited the Earth once during his 108-minute mission.*

The ISS has two bathrooms, a gymnasium and a 360° bay window.

TO THE MOON

To reach the Moon, the US space agency, NASA, developed the *Apollo* spacecraft, part of which, the *Apollo* Lunar Module, ferried 12 astronauts to the Moon's surface between 1969 and 1972.

▲ The Apollo 15 *Command and Service Modules orbit the Moon, awaiting the return of the Lunar Module from the surface.*

A PLACE IN SPACE

A space station is an orbiting spacecraft where astronauts can live and work. The first was *Salyut 1*, in 1971. *The International Space Station* (*ISS*) was pieced together in space during 136 space missions, starting in 1998. The structure has as much space (916 square metres) as a six-bedroomed house and has been occupied since 2000.

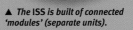

▲ *The ISS is built of connected 'modules' (separate units).*

Around the home

Finding ways to make life easier at home has prompted many domestic inventions. These include ways of cooking and heating, new foods and more effective ways to preserve food so that it can be kept fresh for longer.

▲ An early electric dishwasher used in a hotel kitchen in 1917.

▶ A modern dishwasher dries the plates with hot air.

DISHWASHER

Tired of having crockery chipped by her servants when they did the washing up, Josephine Cochrane devised the first practical dishwashing machine, in 1887. A wooden tub that splashed water onto plates had been patented in 1850 by fellow American Joel Houghton, but Cochrane's device was more effective. A wooden wheel inside a copper boiler was fitted with wire-framed sections to fit dishes. A hand-operated lever turned the wheel and pumped hot, soapy water or clean rinsing water over the dishes.

Central heating
Systems for heating the home were first introduced by the Romans (see page 24).

Flushing toilets
Though invented in the late 16th century, the flushing toilet took years to catch on (see page 25).

Frozen food
Arctic explorers saw how the fast freezing of food preserves its taste (see page 26).

Microwave ovens
Invisible microwaves were first used to cook food in the 1940s (see page 27).

TOAST OF THE TOWN

In the late 19th and early 20th centuries, many machines used electric heating elements to brown bread and turn it into toast. The first pop-up toaster was patented in 1919 by US factory mechanic Charles Strite who fitted a timer and springs to eject the toast when it was done.

▲ *The modern electric toaster has changed little since 1919.*

SUNNY TOAST

In 1990, Americans Simon Hackett and John Romkey demonstrated a toaster that could be controlled from the Internet. Eleven years later, UK engineer Robin Southgate invented a toaster that gathered the weather forecast from the Internet and then toasted the pattern of a cloud, sun or rainfall onto the bread.

▲ *Toast made at the beginning of a sunny day.*

CHOCOLATE TREATS

Chocolate was traditionally taken as a drink until English confectioner Joseph Fry invented the first chocolate bar by mixing cocoa powder and cocoa butter with sugar, in 1847. In the USA, Ruth Wakefield was a dietician and food lecturer who, in 1938, invented cookies baked with chips of chocolate. She sold her chocolate chip cookie idea to food company Nestlé in return for one US dollar and a lifetime's free supply of Nestlé chocolate.

▶ *Chocolate chip cookies were invented when it was found that the chocolate chips did not melt in the short time it took for the dough to bake.*

Vacuum cleaners
These dustbusters use the forces of suction and spinning to clean (see page 28).

Ball point pen
The new writing system made ink smears, smudges and leaks a thing of the past (see page 29).

Light bulbs
The invention of the filament paved the way for the long-lasting lightbulb (see page 30).

Velcro
Sticky seeds provided the inspiration for a new type of clothing fastener (see page 31).

Central heating

For centuries, homes were heated with individual fires in rooms, even though the Romans had developed a central heating system called the hypocaust more than 2000 years earlier.

RADIATORS

A radiator is a metal storage device used to transmit heat generated electrically, or by steam or hot water produced by a boiler. Hot water radiators are common in Europe; steam radiators are more common in North America. In some East Asian countries, the heat from the cooker is used to warm underfloor pipes.

HYPOCAUSTS

A wood-burning furnace stoked by slaves generated heat in a hypocaust. The warm air was channelled underneath the building's floor, which was raised up on pillars made of concrete and layers of tiles, to provide underfloor heating. As warm air rises, channels or spaces left in the building's walls allowed hot air to rise up the building, warming rooms, before it exited the building through openings in the roof called flues.

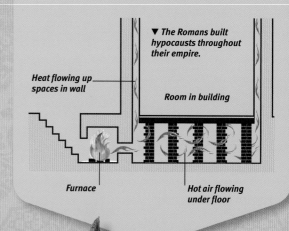

▼ The Romans built hypocausts throughout their empire.

Heat flowing up spaces in wall

Room in building

Furnace

Hot air flowing under floor

◄ A modern radiator has a device called a thermostat that controls its temperature.

HEATING APPS

Today, some homes have central heating that can be controlled remotely from an app on a phone. This means that people can turn on the heating as they leave work, and arrive home to a warm house.

► Using a smartphone's motion sensors, some heating apps can turn the heat up or down in whichever room you're in.

SMART HOME

The radiator was invented by Franz San Galli in a very chilly St Petersburg, Russia, in 1855.

Flushing toilets

Simple flushing toilets existed in some ancient cities more than 4000 years ago. The houses of ancient Minoans on the island of Crete had indoor toilets with drains that were flushed by streams or by hand, using jugs of water.

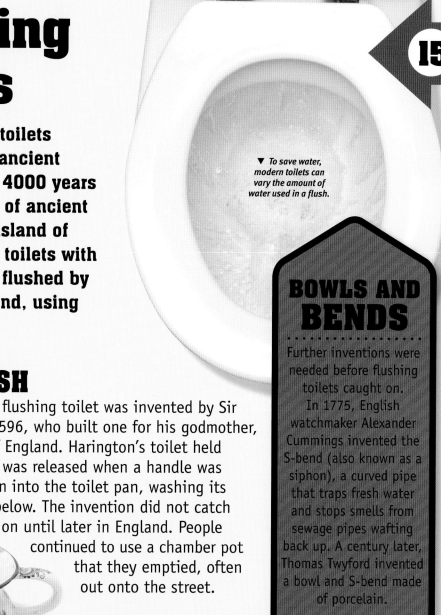

▼ To save water, modern toilets can vary the amount of water used in a flush.

FIRST FLUSH

The first mechanical flushing toilet was invented by Sir John Harington in 1596, who built one for his godmother, Queen Elizabeth I of England. Harington's toilet held water in a tank that was released when a handle was turned. The water ran into the toilet pan, washing its contents into a pit below. The invention did not catch on until later in England. People continued to use a chamber pot that they emptied, often out onto the street.

◄ A Victorian chamber pot, such as this one, was kept under the bed and emptied each morning.

BOWLS AND BENDS

Further inventions were needed before flushing toilets caught on. In 1775, English watchmaker Alexander Cummings invented the S-bend (also known as a siphon), a curved pipe that traps fresh water and stops smells from sewage pipes wafting back up. A century later, Thomas Twyford invented a bowl and S-bend made of porcelain.

NO FLUSHING

Toilets on board spacecraft such as the *International Space Station* (*ISS*) cannot use flushing water as it would float around the craft in microgravity. Instead, they use spinning fans to create an air flow that sucks the waste away. On the *ISS*, the water and solids are separated and the water is cleaned and filtered to be reused as drinking water.

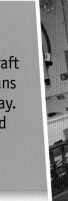

▼ In the space toilet, solids are sucked away by an air flow and freeze dried.

In early space toilets, the freeze-dried solids flaked into bits and floated around the cabin.

Frozen food

Frozen food made Clarence Birdseye very rich. In 1929, he sold his company for $22 million.

26

Clarence Birdseye worked as a naturalist for the US government. While in Canada, in 1912, local Inuit people showed him how fish could be frozen almost instantly under thick ice. Birdseye learned that if food was frozen very fast at very low temperatures of about -40°C, it still tasted fresh when it thawed out.

◄ Clarence Birdseye. was born in 1886. He began his career as a taxidermist – stuffing animals for display.

▼ Frozen blackberries and raspberries

CRYSTALS BIG AND SMALL

For centuries, people had preserved foods by freezing them slowly. This caused large ice crystals to form in the food, so they rarely tasted as good as fresh. Birdseye saw that rapid freezing formed smaller ice crystals inside the food and caused less damage to the food's cells. When the food was then defrosted it had a better taste and texture.

▲ A modern refrigerated vehicle transports frozen foods.

FAST-FREEZE TECHNOLOGY

In the 1920s, Birdseye began testing methods of fast-freezing. Food was packed into waxed cartons and frozen rapidly under pressure, using large metal plates. In 1925, he invented a double-belt freezer that used cold brine (salt water) to chill steel belts, which in turn froze food quickly.

Microwave ovens

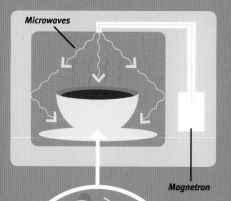

Microwaves

Magnetron

In 1945, US engineer Percy Spencer was working on magnetrons – high-powered **vacuum tubes** – when a bar of chocolate melted in his pocket. Intrigued, he tested an egg, which exploded. The microwaves given off by the magnetrons were quickly cooking the food from within.

◄ A magnetron emits microwaves that are directed into the cooking chamber. Microwaves cause water molecules to vibrate, producing heat.

Water molecule

RADARANGE

Spencer and the company he worked for, Raytheon, patented his idea of a 'RadaRange', which became the first microwave oven in 1946. It was a monster – bulky, heavy and very expensive to buy. Over time, much smaller and cheaper kitchen counter-top versions were developed. By the 1990s, more than nine out of ten US households, for example, had a microwave in their kitchen.

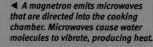

► Standing 1.8 metres tall and weighing 340 kilograms, the 1946 'RadaRange' cost more than £1000.

Do not put a metal object in a microwave oven. It will conduct electricity and sparks will fly!

Vacuum cleaners

In the past, keeping a house clean involved endless sweeping. Rugs were taken outside to have the dust beaten out of them. Much of this hard work disappeared with the arrival of vacuum cleaners in the early 20th century. These devices use fans and air pumps to draw in air, and suck dirt and dust away from surfaces and into a container.

HOW THEY WORK

A rotating brush at the front of the cleaner first loosens dust from the carpet. An electric motor spins a fan that draws in air and dust. The dirty air may pass through filters which let air through but collect hairs and some dust. The air passes into a dust bag or collection chamber where the remaining dust settles, while the cleaner air leaves through a grille.

Dust collection chamber

Electric motor

Fan

Brush

THE FIRST CLEANER

In 1901, Hubert Cecil Booth watched a London railway carriage being cleaned by a machine that forced compressed air out of a hose to blow away dust. Booth's idea was to reverse the action and build a machine with an electric motor that sucked up the dust. His device, the first vacuum cleaner, was too large to fit inside homes. Instead, it was parked outside a house and its giant hoses were carried inside.

▲ *One of Booth's original horse-drawn cleaners.*

PORTABLE POWER

In 1907, US janitor James Spangler built a portable vacuum cleaner out of a tin box, a brush, an electric fan and a pillow case to collect dust. He called it a 'suction sweeper' and in 1908 sold the idea to William Hoover, a leather-goods maker. Hoover produced the machines with such success that they are now associated with his name, not Spangler's.

B llpoint p ns

Writing with ink was a messy business until Hungarian journalist László Bíró invented a new form of pen in 1931. Bíró was frustrated by the way fountain pens leaked and how their ink could smudge on the page because it took so long to dry. He noticed how the thicker, oil-based ink used in newspapers dried almost instantly.

▲ Bíró, the famous inventor of the ballpoint pen, pictured in later life,

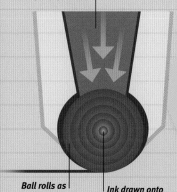

Gravity pulls the ink down and fills the inside face of the ball.

Ball rolls as pen moves.

Ink drawn onto the surface of the ball.

SUPPLYING THE INK

Bíró found that thicker ink would not flow from a fountain pen nib. So he developed a pen with a tiny ball bearing in its tip. As the pen moved across the paper, the ball turned, picking up ink from the cartridge inside the pen. Bíró's 'Eterpen' was first sold in Argentina in 1945. People marvelled at how it wrote without mess and could last for months without refilling. French manufacturer Marcel Bich bought a licence to Bíró's invention and produced his own disposable ballpoint, the 'Bic Cristal', in 1950. Fifty-six years later, the 100 billionth Cristal pen was sold, making it the world's best-selling pen.

GEL PENS

To produce a new form of ink, Japanese company Sakura experimented with more than 1000 different ink ingredients, which included egg whites and grated yam. Their new form of gel ink was water-based, but produced bright colours that didn't fade. Sakura's first gel pens went on sale in 1984.

▶ Gel pens use more ink than ballpoint pens and sometimes smudge on the page. However, they can be used to write or draw finer, more controlled lines.

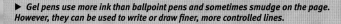

Light bulbs

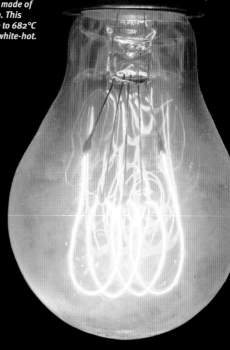

▶ *Modern incandescent light bulbs often use a filament made of tungsten. This heats up to 682°C to glow white-hot.*

Invented in the late 19th century, Incandescent light bulbs use an electric current that passes through a thin filament inside a glass bulb from which the air has been removed. The filament heats up and glows.

KING OF INVENTORS

At his laboratory in Menlo Park, New Jersey, USA, inventor Thomas Edison conducted thousands of experiments to find a long-lasting filament for a light bulb. He gave public demonstrations of his light bulbs in 1879, and in 1880 produced a filament of carbonized bamboo that glowed for 1200 hours. Edison also invented other crucial devices, such as safety fuses, light sockets and voltage regulators.

◀ *Thomas Edison photographed in 1922.*

BRIGHT IDEAS

The air inside early bulbs caused filaments to burn up, so in 1860 English physicist Joseph Swan made the first incandescent bulb with the air removed from inside. In 1879, his bulbs were lighting the first house (his own) and, in 1881, the first public building, London's Savoy Theatre.

▼ *Neon lights are often used in brightly coloured signs.*

IT'S A GAS

When an electric current is passed through neon gas, the two react to produce a bright, orange-red light. The French engineer Georges Claude used this knowledge to invent colourful neon lights in 1910.

Fasteners

After a walk in the Alps in 1941, Swiss engineer Georges de Mestrel noted how the burrs (sticky seeds) of burdock plants stuck to his clothes. He placed burrs under a microscope and saw the hundreds of tiny hooks that caught on to the tiny loops in clothing. This gave him the idea for a fastening device.

◀ Velcro loops

HOOKS AND LOOPS

De Mestral spent years developing an artificial version of the burrs, settling on pairs of nylon strips, one fitted with thousands of hooks that meshed with another strip containing thousands of loops. The challenge of producing a material with 300 tiny hooks per 6.5 sq cm proved daunting, but it was patented in 1955 and called Velcro, from the French words *velours croché* meaning 'hooked velvet'.

In 1968, Puma became the first shoe company to sell trainers with Velcro fasteners.

SAFETY PIN

Brooches have always been used to fasten clothes, but in 1849, US inventor Walter Hunt made a pin from a single piece of wire. It was coiled at one end to form a springy hinge and had a clasp at the other to hold the pin in place. Hunt sold his idea for just a few hundred dollars. The company that bought it made a fortune from selling it worldwide.

▶ Velcro hooks

ZIPS

Seeking a quicker way of getting his boots off, US engineer Whitcomb Judson made a fastener for his footwear. His 1893 invention was a row of eyes and a row of hooks brought together by a metal guide. Judson's invention sold poorly, but an improvement by Gideon Sundback in 1913 became the zip we know today.

Communication

Communication is the sending and receiving of messages. Long ago, people could only do this face-to-face or within shouting or waving distance. Over the centuries, many inventors have come up with ways of communicating over longer distances. Today, we can send messages instantly across the world, and to millions of people at the same time.

The world produces more than 400 million tonnes of paper every single year.

WRITING

A written language allowed people to record facts and ideas. Written words endure much longer than remembered speech. Writing meant that information about laws, history, harvests and taxes could be preserved and read by later generations. The oldest example of written language is on a clay tablet found in the Sumerian city of Uruk (in present-day Iraq) dating from around 3200 BCE.

▲ *The Sumerians pressed signs into soft clay tablets with the end of a wooden tool called a stylus, producing wedge-shaped marks. The tablet was then baked hard.*

Printing press
The invention of movable metal type revolutionized the spread of information (see page 34).

Braille
Louis Braille's system of raised dots allowed the blind to read for the first time (see page 35).

Telegraph
The 1830s saw the first long-distance electrical communication system (see page 36).

Radio
Wireless communication carried by radio waves began in the early 20th century (see page 37).

PICTURE THIS

Some writing systems, such as the hieroglyphs that developed in Egypt from about 3000 BCE onwards, used pictures to represent objects, words and ideas. Hieroglyphs were used by scribes to keep government records. They wrote on thick sheets of papyrus made from pressed marsh reeds. The Maya in Central America also wrote using pictorial writing symbols known as glyphs from around 300 BCE.

▲ *In ancient Egypt, sacred texts were carved in stone, rather than on papyrus.*

PAPER-MAKING

Ts'ai Lun was an official at the Chinese imperial court. In about 105 CE, he invented the first known paper-making process. Plant and cloth fibres were soaked with cleaning agents then rinsed and pounded into a pulp. The pulp was spread over a flat sieve and pressed to squeeze out the water, bonding the fibres to form a single sheet that was then left to dry.

▼ *Images of a Han dynasty woodcut illustrating the five steps in Ts'ai Lun's paper-making process.*

Telephones
Telephones enabled conversations to be carried out over thousands of kilometres (see pages 38–39).

Computers
The history of computing goes all the way from simple adding machines to artificial intelligence (see pages 40–41).

World Wide Web
This invention was sparked by one man's idea of linking information over the Internet (see page 43).

23 # Printing press

The use of carved wooden blocks to print words on paper was first developed in China more than 1000 years ago. However, printing didn't really take off until the mid 15th century when German jeweller Johannes Gutenberg began work on a new type of practical printing press.

▶ In movable type printing, individual metal letters are combined to form the text.

▲ A screw on Gutenburg's press was turned to press the paper onto a frame of type.

METAL MOULDS

Gutenberg completed his printing press in about 1450. He invented movable type made of a metal **alloy** (lead, tin and antimony), which was formed in moulds. Each piece of type was placed in a frame to form a print block that could print a page again and again. He also invented an oily black ink that stuck well to the metal.

PRESS IMPACT

Gutenberg's press did not make him rich, but his invention had a huge impact. Up until this point, books had been expensive and rare because they were individually copied out by hand. The printing press meant that books could be produced quicker and more cheaply than before, allowing major ideas in politics, science and religion to be communicated across countries and continents.

CYLINDER PRESS

German inventors Friedrich Koenig and Andreas Bauer invented the high-speed, steam-powered printing press in 1812. They sold their cylinder press to *The Times* newspaper of London, allowing it to print news far more quickly.

▶ Large, modern newspaper printing presses like this one, are powered by electricity.

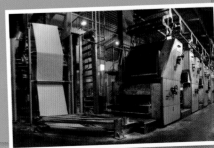

DOT TO DOT

While at the institute, Braille heard about a complex system of 'night writing', designed for the French military which used raised dots and dashes. By 1824, aged just 15, Braille had devised his own simpler system.

It used a two-column grid, each containing between zero and three raised dots. This 6-dot system meant that 63 different combinations were possible – enough for the letters of the alphabet, basic punctuation and the numbers 0 to 9. Braille numbers are the same as the letters A to J, but are preceded by a number symbol.

Braille

Blinded in a childhood accident in 1812, Louis Braille was sent to France's Royal Institute for Blind Youth in Paris. The school's founder, Valentin Haüy, had invented his own books for the visually impaired by **embossing** large letters on pages. Students could read these by tracing the letters' outlines with their fingertips. However, this could be a slow and confusing process, and with such large letters, the books contained little information.

A B C D E F G H I J K L M

N O P Q R S T U V W X Y Z

NUMBER SYMBOL   1 2 3 4 5 6 7 8 9 0

BRAIGO

Braille printers that emboss paper with Braille dots are available, but they are expensive. In 2014, however, 13-year-old Shubham Banerjee from California, USA, developed a small, low-cost Braille printer called Braigo, using the parts of a LEGO Mindstorms kit. Originally designed as a science-fair project, Banerjee has since formed a company to produce Braigo printers.

Telegraph

Before the invention of the electric telegraph in the 1830s, sending a message long distance involved writing a letter, smoke signals or flags waved from hilltops. That was until inventors used an electric battery to send electrical signals long distance along wires.

COOKE AND WHEATSTONE

In 1838, Charles Wheatstone and William Cooke invented the first telegraph system to be used commercially. It went into service on some British railway lines. It used five magnetic needles that could be pointed around a panel of letters and numbers to send an electric signal along wires to a receiving station.

◀ *Wheatstone's five needle telegraph system*

DOTS AND DASHES

In the 1830s, US inventor Samuel Morse developed a code using long and short pulses of electric current to represent different letters of the alphabet. Morse Code became a popular way of communicating over the telegraph services that boomed during the 19th century. By 1851, in the USA alone, 34,000 kilometres of telegraph wire had been laid.

A	B	C
ALFA	BRAVO	CHARLIE

▲ *The Morse Code dots and dashes for letters A, B and C.*

▼ *The ship's designer, Isambard Kingdom Brunel (right) stands next to the ship, the SS Great Eastern, which laid the first successful transatlantic cable.*

LINKING THE WORLD

Use of the telegraph increased rapidly and lines were established all over the world. Europe and North America were linked by telegraph for the first time in 1866 when the first successful under-ocean telegraph cable was laid across the Atlantic, between Canada and Ireland.

In 1900, 63 million telegraph messages were sent in the USA by Western Union alone.

Radio

WIRELESS TELEGRAPH

Convinced that radio waves could be used to carry telegraph messages without needing wires, Marconi developed more powerful versions of his wireless telegraph. In 1901, he made the first successful radio communication across the Atlantic Ocean. The simple signal was three dots – Morse Code for the letter 'S'.

► *British post office engineers test Marconi's wireless telegraphy in 1897.*

Serbian scientist Nikola Tesla and Russian physicist Alexander Popov investigated **radio waves** in the late 19th century. In 1895, a young Italian named Guglielmo Marconi succeeded in sending radio waves over a distance of a kilometre.

STAYING IN TOUCH

Radio waves have transmitted television broadcasts since the 1930s and have allowed space probes to communicate with Earth. Closer to home, radio waves are used over short distances in remote controls and to carry mobile phone voice calls and data.

Nikola Tesla invented the first radio-controlled device, a model boat, in 1898.

RADIO BROADCASTS

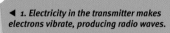

◄ *1. Electricity in the transmitter makes electrons vibrate, producing radio waves.*   ▲ *2. Radio waves travel through the air.*   ► *3. Waves arrive at the receiver, reproducing the original signal.*

Marconi focused on using radio waves to send messages, but others invented radio receivers and transmitters that could send speech and music. In 1907 US inventor Reginald Fessenden made the first sound radio broadcast, which consisted of him talking and playing music. The first radio stations sprang up in North America and Europe in the 1920s.

Telephones

Several inventors – including Antonio Meucci and Elisha Gray – worked on devices that could convert sound waves into electrical signals so that they could be sent down lines. However, it was the Scottish engineer Alexander Graham Bell who patented the first telephone in 1876.

▲ *A model of the first telephone receiver/transmitter, invented by Alexander Graham Bell in 1875.*

BELL'S INVENTION

Bell and his assistant, Thomas Watson, began working on a telephone system while trying to improve the telegraph. In March 1876, Bell made the first telephone call to Watson in another room of their Boston laboratory. The telephone used a cone which collected sound that made a thin membrane and needle vibrate. The moving needle altered the strength of an electric circuit's current. This varying electric current was sent down a wire to a receiving telephone that converted the electric signals back into sound.

▲ *Bell at the opening of the New York–Chicago line in 1892.*

In 2015, the number of mobile phone subscriptions worldwide reached 7 billion.

PHONE EXPLOSION

In 1877, Bell formed a company to build telephones, lines and exchanges that allowed more than one phone to be connected on the same line. In the same year, Thomas Edison also invented a carbon **microphone** that greatly improved sound quality. Telephone use increased, and within a decade there were more than 150,000 telephones in America. By 1910, it was 5.8 million.

▼ Operators at a Bell System telephone switchboard.

SMARTPHONE FIRSTS

▶ Smartphones can be used to access the Internet by means of a touchscreen user interface.

Modern mobile phones can handle computing tasks such as browsing websites and high-quality video recording. Known as smartphones, these devices possess as many as 2000 parts, including a powerful central processing unit (CPU) and a large capacity rechargeable battery. The first Short Message Service (SMS) text message saying 'Merry Christmas' was sent in 1992 over the Vodafone network in the UK. Text messaging has since boomed. Today, more than 400 billion texts are sent worldwide every month.

GOING MOBILE

The first handheld mobile phone was invented by Martin Cooper and his team at the Motorola company in 1973. The prototype weighed a hefty 1.1 kilograms, measured 25 centimetres long and gave 20 minutes talk time after a 10-hour charge of its batteries. It took a decade before the phone would go on sale as the DynaTAC 8000X for a staggering US$3995 – yet demand was high. Rival phones were developed, and advances saw mobile devices shrink in size while increasing their features and battery life.

▲ The DynaTAC 8000x was the first commercial handheld mobile phone.

Computers

Computers are information processing machines. They take in information, via a keyboard, touchscreen or memory stick, then store and process it according to sets of instructions called a computer program. The results are then sent to an output device, such as a monitor or a printer.

▲ *Charles Babbage (1791–1871) invented a machine to perform calculations. His 'Difference Engine' had thousands of mechanical parts but was never completed. However, a replica built by the Science Museum in London in 1991 did work.*

EARLY COMPUTERS

In World War II, scientists tried to calculate weapon paths and crack enemy codes. To help them, engineers built computers to process huge amounts of information by converting them into electrical signals. Vacuum tubes were used to control the flow of these signals through the computers. These vast machines, such as Colossus in Britain, the Zuse Z3 in Germany and ENIAC in the United States, sped up the calculations and paved the way for modern electronic computers.

◄ *The Zuse Z3*

SHRINKING COMPUTERS

As transistors and electronic circuits were shrunk on to silicon chips, computers became smaller, faster, cheaper and more powerful. The first **microprocessor**, a complete computer processing system on a single chip, was developed by Ted Hoff and Federico Faggin in 1971. Microprocessors now power personal computers, smartphones and other computing devices.

COMPUTER PARTS

Modern personal computers are made up of many different parts. These can include:

• CPU board: the microprocessor that instructs other parts of the computers.

• Daughterboard: a small printed circuitboard that allows different components to communicate.

• Graphics card: a piece of hardware that produces the image you see on a monitor.

• Airport: for wireless communication

• Thermal core: conducts heat away from other components.

▲ The interior and components of an Apple mac pro, a modern computer

AirPort card (Bluetooth)

Thermal Core

Fan module

Graphics card

RAM (Random Access Memory) stores data while a computer is performing tasks.

Port board

A CPU (Central Processing Unit) board

Disc-shaped daughterboard

CPU

Outer panel cover

RAM

Graphics card

Flash storage

Logic board

CODING

Before the invention of computer languages, programming a computer to perform a new task often involved rewiring much of the machine. To speed things up, a team led by US programmer Grace Hopper built the first compiler in 1952. This could be programmed with a range of commands which it converted into a code the computer could understand. Compilers enabled high-level programming languages to be developed such as COBOL (Common Business Oriented Language), which made programming faster and more versatile.

SUPERCOMPUTERS

Supercomputers are immensely powerful with thousands of processors used to make vast numbers of calculations for tasks such as weather forecasting. China's Tianhe-2 supercomputer is the world's fastest, capable of making 33,800 trillion calculations per second.

▶ Tianhe-2 is located in the National Supercomputer Centre in Guangzhou, China.

The Internet

Around 205 billion emails were sent every day in 2015 – almost 2.4 million per second.

42

A computer network is a series of computers or digital devices all linked together by cables, phone lines or via wireless radio waves. The Internet is a gigantic network of different computer networks, which share information and talk to each other using common codes and rules.

ARPANET

No one person or single team invented the Internet. It took dozens of scientists and engineers to turn this idea into a reality, which began as a network of just four computers in the USA called ARPANET in 1969. ARPANET allowed military forces and scientists to share information, and grew gradually at first.

◀ *One of the computers that made up the original ARPANET in 1969.*

INTERNET EXPLOSION

In 1985, there were fewer than 5000 devices linked to the Internet. By 2015, this had risen to 16 billion.

EMAIL

The first email was sent over ARPANET by Ray Tomlinson in 1971. He also came up with the idea of using the @ symbol in the email address.

SEARCH ENGINES

The first search engine, Archie, was invented by students Alan Emtage, Bill Heelan and J. Peter Deutsch at Canada's McGill University in 1990.

STREAMING MEDIA

The first ever public stream over the Internet was a live radio broadcast of a baseball game by ESPN SportsZone in 1995.

ENQUIRE

In 1980, a British computer programmer, Tim Berners-Lee, wrote a program called ENQUIRE. It kept track of projects inside CERN – a large European research institute. The program used links between pieces of information called hyperlinks. Clicking on a hyperlink on a computer screen called up another piece of information.

World Wide Web

The World Wide Web (WWW) is a vast collection of different websites available over the Internet. Each website is made up of web pages – documents connected to other pages by links which can be clicked on for easy access.

WELCOME TO THE WEB

In the late 1980s, Berners-Lee began developing a global version of ENQUIRE to work over the Internet on all computers. This involved creating a new computer language, **HTML**, that could be read by all types of machine and **HTTP** – a set of rules to enable webpages to be sent and received. In 1991, the World Wide Web was launched with just one website – a single webpage stored on a computer at CERN.

http://www.

◄ *The name of a website, usually beginning 'http://www', can be typed directly into the address bar of a search engine to go directly to the site.*

In 2014, over 18,000 hours of new videos were added to YouTube every hour.

WEB BOOM

In 1993, CERN announced that the Web would be free for anyone to use. In the same year, Marc Andreessen invented the first browser that could handle graphics and pictures, Mosaic. The number of websites began to grow from just 623 at the end of 1993 to over 900 million in 2016.

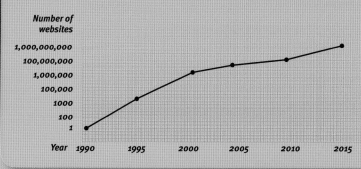

Inventions at work

From the first knives and scrapers made from chipped pieces of flint to tree branches used to lever away obstructions, people have been inventing tools to make work easier for many thousands of years.

▼ The trebuchet was a medieval weapon, a bit like a giant catapult, used for attacking city walls. A heavy weight pulled down a lever to fling rocks or other missiles at the enemy.

Weight

▲ A wooden wedge being used to prise apart a log.

SIMPLE MACHINES

Many early tools and machines were based on simple devices that change the direction or strength of a force. These simple devices include the lever, the screw, the wheel, the wedge and the **pulley**. For instance, the wedge is used in an axe head, while a hammer acts as a lever allowing you to strike objects with extra force.

Batteries
Invented in 1799, these chemical stores of electricity now power many devices (see page 46).

Dynamite
Alfred Nobel's explosive invention is still used in construction (see page 47).

Magnets & Turbines
Electromagnets and steam turbines have been used since the 19th century (see pages 48–49).

Plastics
These versatile materials are used to make everything from furniture to toys (see pages 50–51).

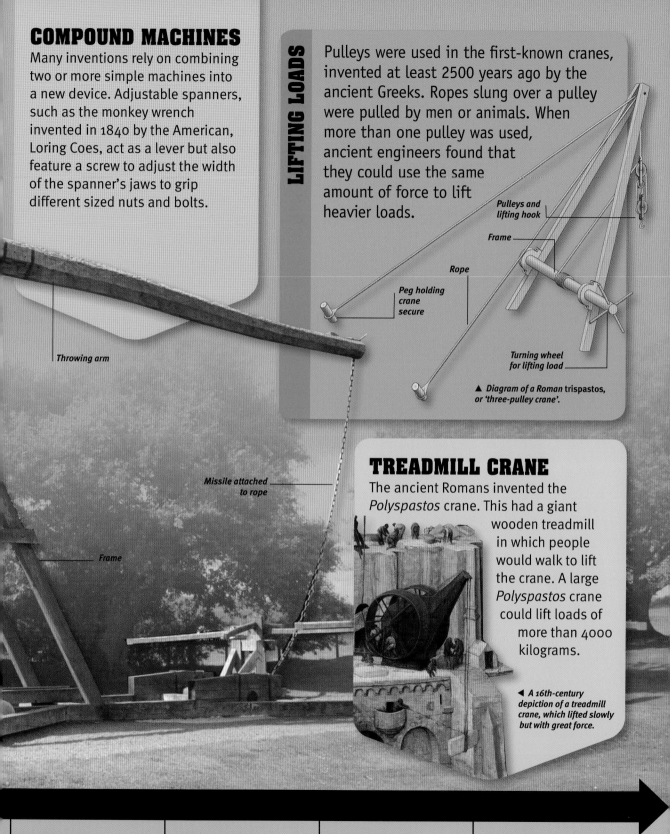

COMPOUND MACHINES

Many inventions rely on combining two or more simple machines into a new device. Adjustable spanners, such as the monkey wrench invented in 1840 by the American, Loring Coes, act as a lever but also feature a screw to adjust the width of the spanner's jaws to grip different sized nuts and bolts.

Throwing arm

LIFTING LOADS

Pulleys were used in the first-known cranes, invented at least 2500 years ago by the ancient Greeks. Ropes slung over a pulley were pulled by men or animals. When more than one pulley was used, ancient engineers found that they could use the same amount of force to lift heavier loads.

Pulleys and lifting hook

Frame

Rope

Peg holding crane secure

Turning wheel for lifting load

▲ Diagram of a Roman trispastos, or 'three-pulley crane'.

Missile attached to rope

Frame

TREADMILL CRANE

The ancient Romans invented the *Polyspastos* crane. This had a giant wooden treadmill in which people would walk to lift the crane. A large *Polyspastos* crane could lift loads of more than 4000 kilograms.

◀ A 16th-century depiction of a treadmill crane, which lifted slowly but with great force.

Transistors
The invention of transistors revolutionized electronic goods (see page 52).

Lasers & robots
The modern inventions of lasers and robots perform tasks that no human being can (see pages 53–55).

Seeing more
Scientists have seen farther using lenses, and even inside the body using X-Rays (see pages 56–59).

Prostheses
Artificial body parts have greatly improved many people's quality of life (see page 61).

Batteries

▲ *A voltaic pile*

A battery is a portable store of chemical energy that can be turned into electricity. Italian scientist Alessandro Volta created the first battery in 1799. His 'voltaic pile' was made up of a stack of alternate disks of zinc, copper and cardboard soaked in salt water. Today, batteries are used to power many objects, from small toys to large cars.

Positive electrode (cathode)

Casing

◄ *More than three billion batteries are sold in the USA every year.*

Electrolyte

Negative electrode (anode)

INSIDE A BATTERY

Modern batteries today look very different from voltaic piles but the principles are the same. Inside lies a positive electrode (cathode) and a negative electrode (anode) made of different materials. Between them is a liquid, powder or paste called an electrolyte. When a battery becomes part of a complete electric circuit, chemical reactions occur inside it. These result in a flow of electrons (tiny parts of atoms) from one electrode to the other, forming an electric current.

BATTERY LIFE

The voltaic pile and many other batteries are known as primary cells. These work until their supply of chemicals runs out. Secondary cells can be recharged and reused many times. Gaston Planté invented the first secondary cell in 1859, using sheets of lead in a solution of sulphuric acid.

▲ *A car battery is a secondary cell.*

Scientists in the USA have made a battery 60,000 times smaller than an AAA battery.

Dynamite

DANGEROUSLY UNSTABLE

Nitroglycerine was first made by Italian chemist Ascanio Sobereo in 1846. This oily liquid proved an extremely powerful explosive – about eight times more powerful than gunpowder. But it was very dangerous and unstable. Even the slightest bump or shock caused it to explode. One such accidental explosion killed Alfred Nobel's brother, Emil, in 1864.

Explosives are used not just in wartime, but also in mining and construction, to blast away rock for tunnels and roads. For centuries, gunpowder was used, but it was relatively weak. In 1869, Swedish chemist Alfred Nobel invented a more powerful explosive that he called dynamite.

Dynamite was originally called 'Nobel's blasting powder'.

MAKING IT SAFE

Alfred Nobel experimented with nitroglycerine on a barge moored in the middle of Lake Mälaren in Sweden. In 1866, he found that mixing the explosive liquid with a chalky sand known as '*kieselguhr*' formed a stable paste. He formed the paste into sticks wrapped with waxed paper that could be transported safely.

▼ A stick of dynamite is fitted with an explosive charge called a blasting cap. When this cap is set off by a burning fuse, it makes the dynamite explode.

NOBEL PRIZES

Nobel made many further inventions including an even more powerful explosive called gelignite. He became extremely wealthy, and left most of his fortune to fund Nobel Prizes for major achievements in physics, chemistry, literature, peace and medicine.

◄ Alfred Nobel

Electromagnets

In 1820, Danish scientist Hans Christian Ørsted noticed how a compass needle moved away from pointing north whenever a battery-powered electric circuit was switched on. He had discovered that when an electric current flows in a wire it creates a magnetic field around the wire – the key principle behind electromagnets.

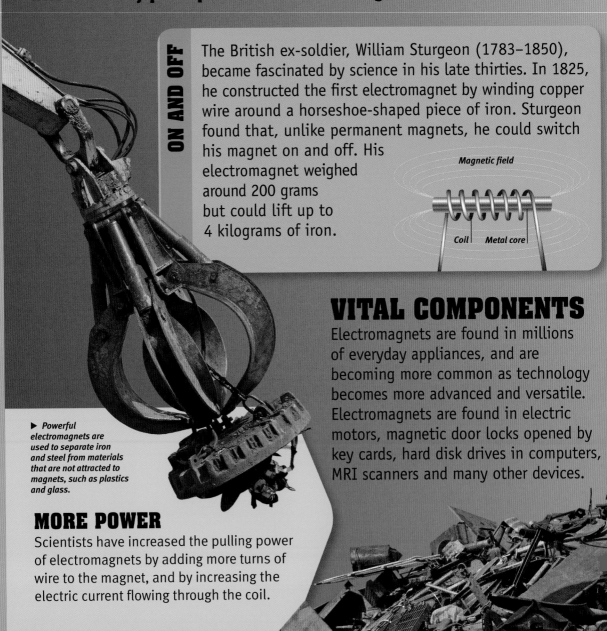

Maglev trains use magnetic levitation to float above the tracks.

ON AND OFF

The British ex-soldier, William Sturgeon (1783–1850), became fascinated by science in his late thirties. In 1825, he constructed the first electromagnet by winding copper wire around a horseshoe-shaped piece of iron. Sturgeon found that, unlike permanent magnets, he could switch his magnet on and off. His electromagnet weighed around 200 grams but could lift up to 4 kilograms of iron.

Magnetic field

Coil   *Metal core*

VITAL COMPONENTS

Electromagnets are found in millions of everyday appliances, and are becoming more common as technology becomes more advanced and versatile. Electromagnets are found in electric motors, magnetic door locks opened by key cards, hard disk drives in computers, MRI scanners and many other devices.

▶ *Powerful electromagnets are used to separate iron and steel from materials that are not attracted to magnets, such as plastics and glass.*

MORE POWER

Scientists have increased the pulling power of electromagnets by adding more turns of wire to the magnet, and by increasing the electric current flowing through the coil.

Steam turbines

▼ Sir Charles Parsons

A turbine is a spinning wheel, often made up of lots of blades that are turned by a gas or liquid. The Anglo-Irish engineer, Sir Charles Parsons, devised a new way of generating electricity by using steam to drive turbines which, in turn, moved the parts of a generator to produce electricity.

POWER GENERATOR

Parsons' first steam turbine generator, completed in 1884, generated just 7.5 kilowatts of electricity, but he quickly built more powerful models. In 1890, the Forth Bank Power Station opened in Newcastle – the first to generate electricity using steam turbines. Many more followed, as people found that Parsons' invention allowed electricity to be generated quickly and efficiently. Today, steam turbines account for around 80 per cent of the electricity generated in power stations, using coal, oil or nuclear power to heat water into steam.

▼ Modern steam turbines found in some power stations can generate 1.5 gigawatts of power – equivalent to the power of 20,000 small cars.

SPEED SHIP

Parsons also invented the first steam turbine-powered ship, the *Turbinia*, in 1894. Fitted with three steam turbines that drove nine propellers, the 32-metre-long ship managed speeds of over 34 knots (63 kilometres per hour) – making it the fastest in the world. As a result, many large battleships and cruise liners adopted steam turbines as their power plants.

▼ The Turbinia at sea in 1897.

RMS *Mauretania* and HMS *Dreadnought* were powered by turbines developed by Parsons.

Plastics

Plastics are a group of materials made of long chains of molecules known as polymers, which can be moulded and shaped under heat and pressure. Plastics are often lightweight and cheap to produce with many useful properties. Over 300 million tonnes of plastics are produced each year for a wide range of products, including toys, furniture and clothing.

NATURAL PLASTICS

Materials exist in nature that are plastic. These include tortoise shell, ivory from elephant's tusks and rubber. Attempts to create an alternative material to ivory led to Alexander Parkes inventing Parkesine – a plastic made from cellulose found in plant fibres. John and Isaiah Hyatt bought the patent for Parkesine, and in the 1860s developed their own cellulose-based plastic, which they called **celluloid**.

◀ *Celluloid was used to make billiard balls, false teeth and clear, flexible photographic film for use in photography and the early movie industry.*

BAKELITE

Belgium-born chemist Leo Baekeland invented a pioneering new plastic in 1907 using substances extracted from oil. The resulting material, called Bakelite, was the first **synthetic** plastic – one not made from plants or animals, but from chemicals and fossil fuel products. It was also the first thermosetting plastic (a plastic that does not soften when heated). Today, most plastics are produced from oil.

◀ *Bakelite was the standard material for making telephones during the 1930s and 1940s.*

NYLON

Seeking an alternative to natural silk, American chemist Wallace H. Carrothers developed a new plastic fibre that was introduced as nylon in 1938. Nylon was tough, resistant to wear and was originally used to replace silk in stockings and parachute canopies. It is now used for thousands of different products, such as cookware, clothing and plastic gears.

▼ *In the years following World War II, most of the nylon produced was used in the manufacture of tights.*

AMAZING NEW CONCEPT IN *Cooking*

FREE SPATULA WITH EACH "HAPPY PAN"

NOTHING STICKS TO 'HAPPY PAN'

A cast iron skillet sealed with DuPont TEFLON®

▲ *In 1961, DuPont unveiled the 'Happy Pan', a Teflon coated frying pan.*

TEFLON

In 1938, 27-year-old American chemist, Roy Plunkett, was trying to develop a new fridge coolant for DuPont when he discovered a white waxy powder in his laboratory equipment. The material did not react with other chemicals and was extremely slippery. These properties have made it excellent as a non-stick coating for cookware, and it is also used in many industrial products, including bearings.

STYROFOAM

Invented in 1941, Styrofoam is polystyrene plastic full of air bubbles (it's about 98 per cent air). Lightweight, highly buoyant and a good heat insulator, one of its first uses was in a United States Coastguard lifeboat in 1942. It is used in sheets for insulating buildings, packaging goods, and in disposable cups and plates.

◄ *These small pieces of packaging styrofoam are known as 'peanuts'.*

KEVLAR

The American polymer scientist Stephanie Kwolek (1923–2014), developed a new plastic, Kevlar, in 1965 that is light but incredibly strong – more than eight times stronger than steel, but just a fifth of its weight. Kevlar is used to make spacesuits, suspension bridges, body armour and many other things.

▼ *Because of its lightness and strength, Kevlar is found in many vehicles, such as racing cars, aircraft and boats.*

Transistors

Vacuum tubes were invented in 1907 by John Ambrose Fleming. They were used as switches to control electrical signals and were a mainstay of electronic products in the early 20th century. In 1947, three engineers at Bell Labs in the USA invented the **transistor**. John Bardeen, Walter Brattain, and William Shockley's device was far smaller, more reliable and used a lot less power than vacuum tubes.

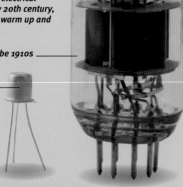

▶ A vacuum tube shown dwarfing a transistor. Vacuum tubes were used in electrical devices in the early 20th century, but needed time to warm up and often overheated.

Vacuum tube 1910s

Transistor 1950s

SHRINKING TECHNOLOGY

The invention of transistors meant that electrical goods could be built cheaper, smaller and often worked better than before. The first transistor radio, the Regency TR-1, went on sale in the US in 1954. A boom in electronic consumer goods followed.

▶ Thanks to integrated circuit technology, it is now possible to fit a computer's entire CPU (central processing unit) onto a single chip.

INTEGRATED CIRCUITS

Transistors shrank in size from the earliest models, which were a few centimetres long, to ones measuring just a fraction of a millimetre. In the late 1950s, researchers managed to etch complete electronic circuits containing many transistors onto tiny fingernail-sized wafers of material. These integrated circuits allowed faster, more powerful – and smaller – computers to be produced.

LIGHT WORK

Many types of laser have been invented which today perform an incredibly wide range of tasks from carrying information along fibre optic cables to reading DVDs in a media player.

CUTTING

Powerful industrial lasers can cut through the toughest materials or work with pinpoint precision to etch out the electric circuits of a circuit board used in electronics.

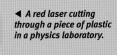

◀ *A red laser cutting through a piece of plastic in a physics laboratory.*

▼ *Laser eye surgery has become increasingly common in recent years.*

CORRECTING

Lasers are used in medicine where they can correct certain eye problems, seal blood vessels during surgery or cut out and destroy diseased cells.

MEASURING

Lasers are used to measure distances in construction and the speed of passing vehicles by police officers.

▶ *This tool uses a laser to measure if something, such as a shelf, is level.*

Lasers

Lasers are powerful, focused beams of light. In 1960, the American scientist, Theodore H. Maiman built the first working laser, using a photographer's flash lamp. Inside the lamp, Maiman placed a rod made of ruby crystal which produced a narrow beam of red light when the flash lamp was fired.

HOW LASERS WORK

Most lasers are tubes that have mirrors at both ends and contain a crystal, gas or liquid. When a lamp or some other device adds energy to the tube's contents, their atoms get excited and generate light. This is bounced between the mirrors in the tube, which increases its power before it exits through the front mirror as a narrow beam of laser light.

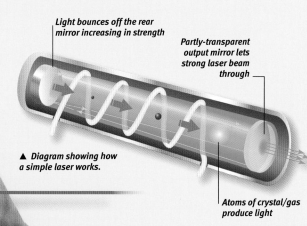

Light bounces off the rear mirror increasing in strength

Partly-transparent output mirror lets strong laser beam through

▲ *Diagram showing how a simple laser works.*

Atoms of crystal/gas produce light

Robots

Robots are machines that can perform precise, repetitive tasks that are too hard or dangerous for people. Most robots can respond to their surroundings and can be programmed to perform a range of jobs.

INDUSTRIAL ROBOTS

The first robot that served an industrial purpose was *Unimate*, built by inventors George Devol and Joseph Engelberger. This 4-tonne robotic arm went to work in 1961 in car factories in the United States, where it handled red-hot metal castings. Other robot arms followed, capable of spray-painting products, handling goods and welding parts of cars together with great accuracy. More than a million robots now work in all kinds of industries worldwide.

PARTS OF A ROBOT

Controllers are the 'brains' of a robot. They make decisions and instruct the robot's parts to move in specific ways. Controllers can be programmed by humans to perform different jobs. Drive systems provide the power to move a robot's parts. Some robots are powered by electric motors. Others use compressed air or hydraulics. Sensors are devices such as cameras, microphones and light detectors that gather data about the robot's surroundings and send it back to the controller. End effectors are parts, such as a hand or magnetic gripper, that move objects or interact with a robot's surroundings.

▼ *Developed by NASA, the Curiosity rover is the size of a small car and is powered by a thermoelectric generator. It reached Mars in 2012 after a 560-million-kilometre journey from Earth.*

ROBOTIC EXPLORERS

Robots can explore places too dangerous for humans. NASA's *Sojourner* rover was the first robot to move across another planet when it explored Mars in 1997. In 1994, the *Dante II* robot climbed inside an active volcano, while in 2013, a tiny robot called *Tlaloc II-TC* discovered chambers underneath an ancient temple in Mexico.

◀ The **ABB IRB 340 FlexPicker** *industrial robot can handle up to 150 objects per minute – far faster than a human worker.*

HUMANOIDS

The first full-size robot that was designed to look and act like a human was *Wabot-1*. It was created in 1970 by a team at Japan's Waseda University led by Ichiro Kato. Humanoid robots have since worked as museum guides and even ventured into space (*Robonaut 2*). Some, like *NAO*, use cameras and programs in their controllers to recognize different human faces.

▶ *Honda first demonstrated its ASIMO humanoid robot in 2000. Fitted with 34 small electric motors, it can climb up and down stairs and run at speeds of 6 kilometres per hour.*

TO THE RESCUE

Robots have been developed to aid rescue workers at disaster sites. Invented in 2004, Tmsuk's *T52-Enryu* is a giant twin-armed robot able to clear debris and rescue people. Each arm is 6 metres long and can lift 500 kilograms. Its hydraulic drive system gives it enough power to rip a car door off its hinges.

Zooming in

Lenses made of polished glass were first made into spectacles in Italy in the 13th Century. Before then, Middle Eastern scholars had noticed how pieces of glass could bend light to make objects appear closer. Dutch lens makers in the late 16th and early 17th century would combine lenses to form the first microscopes and telescopes.

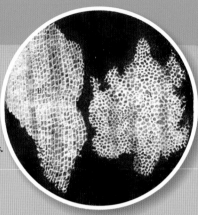

▶ In 1665, the English scientist, Robert Hooke, published the first illustrations of objects, such as these cork cells, observed under microscopes.

SEEING SMALL THINGS

Dutch father and son Hans and Zaccharias Janssen placed lenses in tubes in the 1590s to invent the first microscopes. These were considered novelties and could magnify objects only about nine or ten times. But another Dutchman, Anton Van Leeuwenhoek, was able to produce much more powerful lenses. By the 1670s, he had made microscopes with 270 times magnification, becoming the first person to view bacteria and sperm.

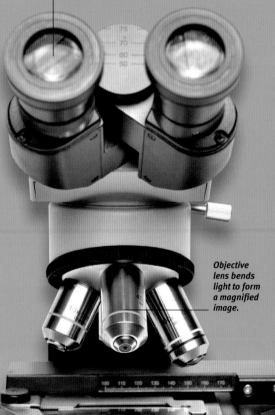

Eyepiece contains a lens which further magnifies the focused image from the objective lens.

Objective lens bends light to form a magnified image.

SEEING WITH BEAMS

Ernst Ruska, a German physicist, invented the first electron microscope in 1933. Instead of light, it beamed a stream of tiny particles called electrons at objects. It could achieve incredible magnifications of more than 50,000 times, allowing individual atoms and molecules to be seen.

◀ In an optical microscope, the objective lens (or lenses) focuses light shining through the specimen (the object being studied) to form a magnified image.

Specimen holder

MIRROR, MIRROR

In 1668, the English physicist, Sir Isaac Newton, came up with a new design – the reflecting telescope. It used mirrors to capture light and then direct it to a person's eye, and could achieve 40 times magnification. Because larger mirrors are less tricky to make than large lenses, most major optical telescopes today are **reflectors** rather than **refractors**.

▲ *Sir Isaac Newton (1642–1726), inventor of the reflecting telescope.*

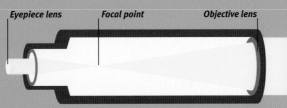

Eyepiece lens   Focal point   Objective lens

◄ **Light is bent by the objective lens and then magnified by the eyepiece lens.**

REFRACTING TELESCOPE

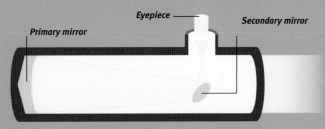

Eyepiece   Secondary mirror

Primary mirror

◄ **Light is focused by the primary mirror and then bounced off a secondary mirror towards the eyepiece.**

REFLECTING TELESCOPE

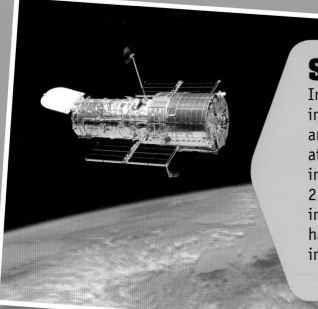

▲ *Hubble telescope in space*

SPACE TELESCOPES

In recent times, telescopes have been sent into space where they can observe stars and galaxies 24 hours a day without Earth's atmosphere getting in the way. Launched in 1990, the *Hubble Space Telescope* has a 2.4-metre reflector telescope, scientific instruments and digital cameras which have taken more than 700,000 detailed images of objects in space.

Seeing inside the body

In 1895, German physicist Wilhelm Röntgen was experimenting with light tubes filled with gas when he discovered, by accident, mysterious waves of energy. He found that they passed through soft parts of the body, but not through metal or bones. He named them X-rays.

▲ *German physicist Wilhelm Röntgen was the discoverer of X-rays. His achievement transformed physics and medical practice.*

CAPTURED ON FILM

To prove his discovery, Röntgen placed a photographic plate behind his wife's hand resulting in the first ever X-ray radiogram. It showed clearly the bones of the fingers normally hidden by the skin and flesh. Radiographic departments sprang up in hospitals and medical centres using X-rays, and Röntgen received the first ever Nobel Prize for Physics in 1901.

CT SCANNERS

Invented in 1971 by a British electrical engineer named Godfrey Hounsfield, CT (computerized tomography) scanners take X-rays from several different positions. These images are then processed by a computer to build up a detailed 3D picture of the relevant body part, such as the skull.

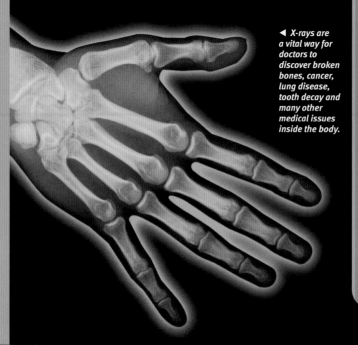

◀ *X-rays are a vital way for doctors to discover broken bones, cancer, lung disease, tooth decay and many other medical issues inside the body.*

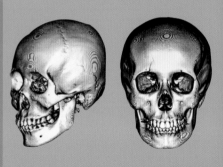

▲ *CT scans showing two views of the human skull.*

X-rays are used in airport security scanners to check the contents of bags.

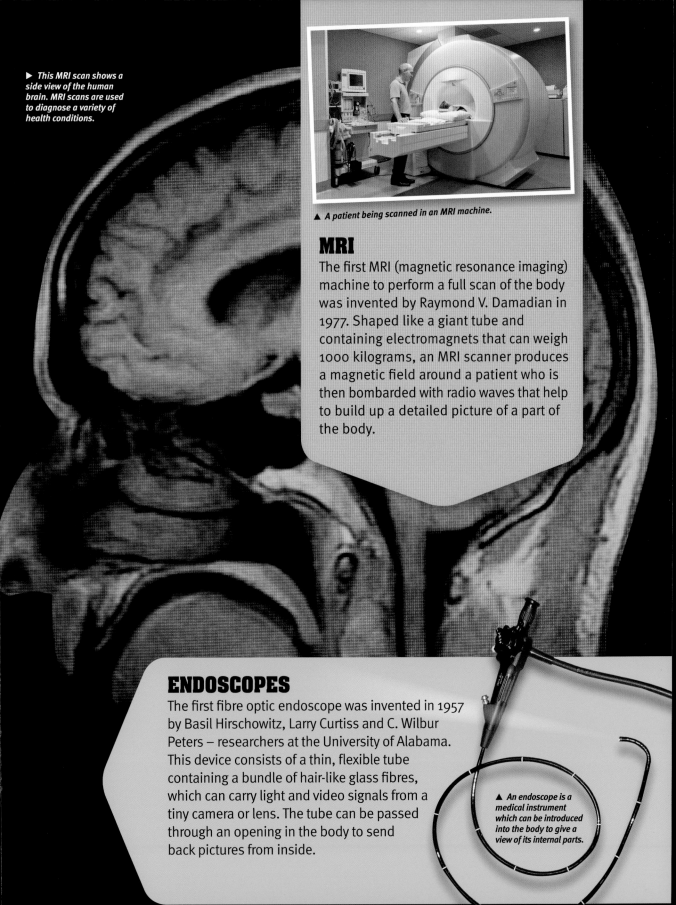

▶ This MRI scan shows a side view of the human brain. MRI scans are used to diagnose a variety of health conditions.

▲ A patient being scanned in an MRI machine.

MRI

The first MRI (magnetic resonance imaging) machine to perform a full scan of the body was invented by Raymond V. Damadian in 1977. Shaped like a giant tube and containing electromagnets that can weigh 1000 kilograms, an MRI scanner produces a magnetic field around a patient who is then bombarded with radio waves that help to build up a detailed picture of a part of the body.

ENDOSCOPES

The first fibre optic endoscope was invented in 1957 by Basil Hirschowitz, Larry Curtiss and C. Wilbur Peters – researchers at the University of Alabama. This device consists of a thin, flexible tube containing a bundle of hair-like glass fibres, which can carry light and video signals from a tiny camera or lens. The tube can be passed through an opening in the body to send back pictures from inside.

▲ An endoscope is a medical instrument which can be introduced into the body to give a view of its internal parts.

Medical inventions of the past 250 years have saved and improved millions of patients' lives. These have ranged from new drugs to prevent or fight infections to the stethoscope, invented by Frenchman René Laennec in 1816. This instrument allows doctors to listen to the beating hearts and lungs of patients as they breathe.

ANTISEPTICS

It was only 150 years ago that scientists realized that the cause of many infections and diseases was microscopic living things such as bacteria. Until that time, operations were often carried out in dirty conditions. British surgeon Joseph Lister began using phenol (then called carbolic acid) to clean wounds and kill off bacteria in 1865. It was the first **antiseptic** and helped to dramatically reduce the numbers of people who died from infections after surgery.

▼ *Lister cleaned medical instruments with carbolic acid and even sprayed entire operating theatres to keep things clean.*

PACEMAKERS

Some people's hearts do not beat regularly. They can be fitted with an artificial pacemaker that helps the heart keep a healthy rhythm by sending small electrical pulses to stimulate the heart's muscles into beating. Early pacemakers were large machines that sat outside of the body, but in 1958 the Swede, Rune Elmqvist, designed the first pacemaker that could be implanted inside the patient.

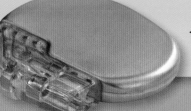

◄ *Modern pacemakers measure just a few centimetres across.*

Artificial body parts made for animals have included an eagle's beak and a dolphin's tail.

STICKING PLASTERS

Earle Dickson worked for a bandage and dressings manufacturer. In 1920, after realising how even the smallest cut required someone's help to apply a bandage, he invented self-sticking plasters. He cut small squares of bandage to which he affixed sticking tape. Dickson's convenient invention, which helps prevent infection, went on sale that year under the name Band-Aid.

ARTIFICIAL BODY PARTS

Prostheses are artificial devices used to replace a part of the body that is missing or does not work well. The oldest known prosthesis is an artificial toe made of wood and leather found on an Ancient Egyptian mummy that's at least 2700 years old.

ARTIFICIAL HEART

The Jarvik 7 was the first artificial heart to be successfully transplanted inside a human patient in 1982. It was invented by American doctors, Robert Jarvik and Willem Johan Kolff.

▲ An artificial heart from the 1990s.

I-LIMB

Invented by David Gow in 2007, the I-Limb was the first artificial hand to feature five independently powered fingers. This allowed it to grip and manipulate objects like a real hand.

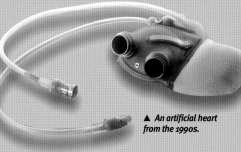

▶ The I-Limb is among the most advanced artificial body parts yet invented.

HIP REPLACEMENT

Worn-out hip ball-and-socket joints can be replaced with a complete artificial hip joint following pioneering work by British surgeon Sir John Charnley in the 1950s and 1960s.

That's entertainment

Many inventors have come up with devices that entertain and amuse people. Sometimes, these inventions are new twists or improvements on existing objects. For example, Theobald Boehm took the traditional wooden flute and by 1847 had developed a louder metal version with moveable keys that made the instrument easier to play.

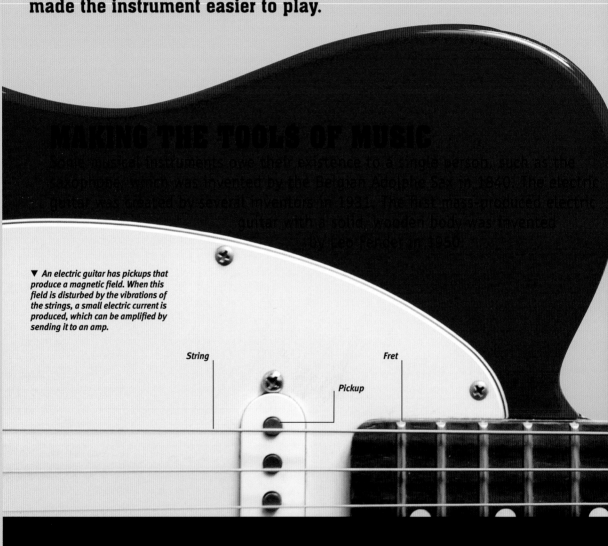

MAKING THE TOOLS OF MUSIC

Some musical instruments owe their existence to a single person, such as the saxophone, which was invented by the Belgian Adolphe Sax in 1840. The electric guitar was created by several inventors in 1931. The first mass-produced electric guitar with a solid, wooden body was invented by Leo Fender in 1950.

▼ An electric guitar has pickups that produce a magnetic field. When this field is disturbed by the vibrations of the strings, a small electric current is produced, which can be amplified by sending it to an amp.

String

Fret

Pickup

Early photographs required the subject to stay perfectly still for 60 to 90 seconds.

62

Moving pictures
The cinema industry was born in France at the end of the 19th century. (see pages 64–65).

Recording sounds
From phonographs to MP3s, recording methods have become ever more advanced (see pages 66-67).

Television
Various inventors created different television systems in the 1920s and 30s (see pages 68–69).

Trampolines
This bouncy leisure device was invented by a teenage gymnast (see page 70).

EARLY PHOTOGRAPHY

An 1826 image captured by the Frenchman Nicéphore Niépce on a pewter plate covered in a light-sensitive coating of bitumen is considered the first photograph. A friend of Niépce's, Louis Daguerre, produced the first commercial photos, known as daguerreotypes', on thin copper sheets coated in silver in 1839.

▼ One of the earliest daguerrotypes showing a Parisian street in 1839.

THE BOX BROWNIE

American inventor George Eastman developed the first photographic film made from celluloid in 1889. In 1900, his company released the first simple and cheap camera, the Box Brownie, for just $1. It took pictures measuring 5.7 centimetres square.

► Millions of Box Brownies were sold.

BARBIE

The American Ruth Handler invented this plastic doll in 1959 after watching her daughter, Barbara, playing with paper dolls. By 2002, more than a billion Barbies had been sold.

► A Barbie is sold every 3 seconds.

SNAP HAPPY

Digital cameras don't use film. Instead, they store the images in their memory. The first, invented in 1975 by Steve Sasson, took 23 seconds to record each single picture to magnetic tape. Modern digital cameras can store thousands of images on small memory cards.

▲ The first digital camera weighed 3.6 kg.

Video games
First devised on university campuses, video games have become one of the world's most popular forms of entertaiment (see pages 72–73).

Nanotechnology
Development of the world's smallest machines may lead to medical breakthroughs in the future (see page 74).

3D printing
Objects built by 3D printers are already being used in cars, planes and many other applications (see page 75).

Moving pictures

In the 19th century, scientists discovered that an image viewed by the eye stays in the brain for a fraction of a second after the image has gone. Inventors exploited this principle to flick or spin a series of drawings – each drawing slightly different than the last – past the eye. If viewed at the right speed, the brain interprets the pictures as a continuous, moving image.

EARLY DEVICES

Early moving picture devices included the thaumatrope, invented by John Ayrton Paris in 1824. It spun different images on either side of a card to provide what appears to be a combined image. Eadweard Muybridge invented the Zoopraxiscope in 1879, a device that projected sequences of images from spinning glass discs to give the illusion of a moving scene.

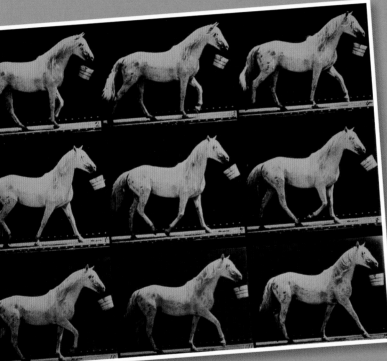

◀ *Muybridge photographed horses in sequence, so that when projected by the Zoopraxiscope they gave the illusion of movement.*

MAKING MOVIES

1940
THE THIEF OF BAGHDAD

The Thief of Baghdad used blue screen technology, when actors perform in front of a blue background, upon which background images are later added.

1952
BWANA DEVIL

Bwana Devil, the first colour 3D movie, was viewed by audience members who wore glasses with different coloured lenses to enjoy the 3D effect.

William Dickson, working for Thomas Edison, developed the Kinetoscope between 1888 and 1892. Inside a wooden box, a battery-powered electric motor ran a spool of photographic film past a peephole, through which a single audience member could view an impression of a continuous moving scene.

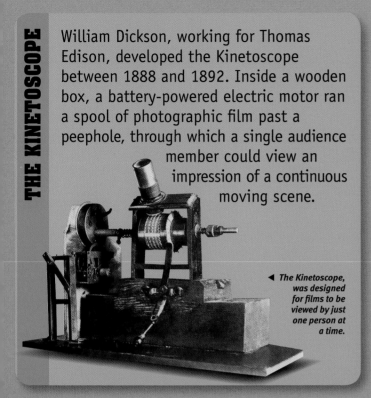

◄ The Kinetoscope, was designed for films to be viewed by just one person at a time.

▶ An actress demonstrates how to speak into an early boom microphone.

THE TALKIES

Talking films arrived in 1927 with *The Jazz Singer* – the first major movie using the Vitaphone sound system invented by Western Electric. It recorded the soundtrack of a film onto discs 40 centimetres in diameter. When the projector started, it spun a linked record turntable to play the soundtrack in time with the pictures.

▼ The Cinématographe motion picture camera was invented in the 1890s.

BIRTH OF CINEMA

Brothers Auguste and Louis Lumière had seen a Kinetoscope at an exhibition in Paris and were inspired to invent their own movie system. Their Cinématographe device worked both as a movie camera and as a projector. They used 35 mm film that displayed 16 separate photos every second and could be viewed by more than one person at the same time.

IMAX®

1975
STEADICAM

Invented by Garrett Brown, the Steadicam support system allows shake-free filming. Early uses included *Return of the Jedi*.

1986
IMAX 3D

The first IMAX 3D cinema was built in Vancouver, Canada, and showed widescreen 3D films.

1995
COMPUTER ANIMATION

Pixar's *Toy Story* was the first full-length film to be completely animated by computer.

Sound recording

Sound waves travel as vibrations through the air or another medium, varying in amplitude (loudness) and frequency (highness or lowness). Thomas Edison was the first inventor to capture, store and replay sound with the invention of his phonograph in 1877. It was Edison's favourite among all his many inventions.

THE PHONOGRAPH

Edison's phonograph used a horn to gather sound, which caused a metal stylus to vibrate. This stylus etched a series of small indentations onto a thin sheet of tin foil wrapped around a brass cylinder which was turned by a handle. When the cylinder with the indentations was replayed, the stylus's vibrations were amplified by the horn to create audible sound.

◄ *Edison's tinfoil recordings wore out quickly, but in the mid-1880s, wax cylinders were invented which were more durable. However, these wax cylinders had to be recorded one at a time.*

RECORD MAKER

In 1887, the German-American, Emile Berliner, invented a way of producing multiple copies of recorded sound using a flat disc. A master disc of zinc was used to press copies of the disc out of rubber and, later, vinyl plastic. Each disc contained a long spiral track full of tiny bumps which caused the stylus to vibrate and create sound waves when the disc was spun. Berliner called the device the gramophone and the discs became known as records.

▼ *Gramophone records from 1908.*

GOING DIGITAL

Digital sound involves sampling sound waves in order to convert them into a stream of code that can be stored as an electronic file. The first popular digital recorded sound format was the compact disc (CD) developed by two large electronics companies, Phillips and Sony. On sale since 1982, each CD was read by a laser inside a CD player which turned the data into electric signals that could become sounds waves. CDs were less delicate than vinyl records, offered good quality sound and users could jump to individual tracks in any order.

◀ *Edison pictured with his phonograph in 1878.*

▶ *A standard CD is 120 mm in diameter and holds up to 80 minutes of sound on a spiral track that if stretched out in a line would measure 5.6 km.*

MP3

MP3 is a type of computer file for storing sound information. Developed in Germany in the 1980s, it compresses all the sound data so that it takes up less memory space on a computer or other digital device, with only a small loss of sound quality. MP3 compression works by not including sounds too low or too high-pitched for humans to typically hear. It also does not include sounds which are masked (drowned out) by other sounds in a track. The resulting file can be just a tenth of the size of the original, making it quicker to download over the Internet.

MP3 PLAYERS

The first portable MP3 player was the MPMan F10 launched in 1998 by the Korean company, SaeHan Information Systems. Its 32 Mb memory could hold only around 10 to 20 songs. Today, many music lovers listen to digital sound on their smartphones or digital musical players, which can hold thousands of songs with ease.

◀ *Launched in 2001, the Apple iPod became the most successful MP3 player.*

Television

The invention of the television was the work of many individuals. All television systems rely on three key parts: cameras to capture moving images; transmission systems to broadcast the images as signals by cable, satellite or through the air; and television sets to receive and display the images.

FIRST TV IMAGES

German engineer Paul Nipkow invented a spinning disc with small holes in 1884 that could scan an image and convert it into electric signals (above). Scottish inventor, John Logie Baird used the disc to build a mechanical television set in 1924. The following year, Baird gave the first public demonstration of moving images on a television screen in a London department store.

◄ Vladimir Zworykin demonstrates his electronic television system in 1929.

ELECTRONIC TV

While John Logie Baird persisted with mechanical television, a Russian living in America, Vladimir Zworykin, and a young American, Philo Farnsworth, both envisaged all-electronic systems that used **cathode ray tubes** for both transmitting and receiving images. Electronic TVs won out over mechanical models in the late 1930s because they could produce bigger, clearer images with more detail.

By 2009, more than half of all US homes had three or more televisions.

IN COLOUR

In 1946, there were only 8000 US households with television. By 1962, 49 million homes had them. Nearly all were black-and-white, even though colour TV had appeared in the early 1950s. As the price of colour TV sets dropped and the number of shows broadcast in colour rose, so did colour TV ownership. By 1970, there were over 23 million colour TVs in the USA.

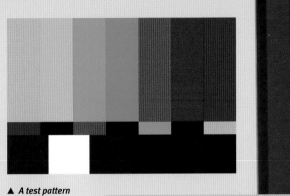

▲ A test pattern used to be broadcast at times when the transmitter was active but no programme was being shown.

FLAT SCREEN TV

Bulky cathode ray tubes began to be replaced by flat-screen TVs from the late 1980s. Flat-screen TVs consume less power, and their display is made up of thousands of tiny cells called pixels. A TV signal instructs all the different pixels in a flat screen to be lit in different colours in order to form the image on screen. High definition (HD) TV uses lots of pixels to produce a sharper, clearer TV picture. The first HD broadcasts in Europe were of the 1990 FIFA World Cup, produced by the Italian broadcaster, RAI.

REMOTE CONTROL

The first wireless remote controller was invented in 1955 by Eugene Polley. The Flash-Matic shone a beam of light at televisions fitted with simple light sensors called photo cells. It allowed people to change channels and sound levels without leaving their seats. Most modern remotes send a beam of invisible infrared light to the TV.

▲ The Flash-Matic

▲ Modern remote controllers have many buttons for changing different settings .

Trampolines

In 1930, 16-year-old gymnast George Nissen watched as some trapeze artists bounced up and down in their safety net after dismounting. Inspired, he invented his own 'bouncing rig' in his family's garage in Iowa. It was made of canvas stretched over a frame made of old iron bars and held in place by rubber inner tubes from tyres.

REBOUND RESEARCH

In 1936, University of Iowa gymnastics coach Larry Griswold worked with Nissen to refine the bouncing rig's design. They used coiled springs to attach the canvas sheet to the frame. This gave the bed more bounciness. The pair formed a company to build and sell trampolines in 1942.

▲ Modern trampolines use strips of strong, stretchy fabric woven together.

▲ Nissen developed a sport using trampolines, called Space ball.

BOUNCING BACK

Nissen had initially thought that trampolines would be used just by gymnasts and acrobats, but trampolining soon became a popular leisure pursuit in the United States and around the world. Nissen spent much of the rest of his life demonstrating and promoting trampolining as a sport.

Snowboards

On Christmas Day, 1965, the American engineer Sherman Poppen had an idea. To keep his two daughters amused, he bound two children's skis together to create a flat board that the girls could stand on to slide down the snow-covered hills near their home in Michigan. The sport of snowboarding had begun.

▶ A modern snowboard with velcro foot bindings.

BOARD TALK

Poppen developed his design, making a board shorter and wider than the original skis and fitting pads to help shoes grip the board. He also added a rope to the front for steering. He patented the idea in 1966 as a 'Surf-Type Snow Ski'. However, his wife, Nancy, suggested he call this early type of snowboard a Snurfer, from the words, 'snow' and 'surfer'. Poppen licensed Snurfers to a company, Brunswick, which sold over 300,000 in the first year.

IN A BIND

In the late 1970s, keen Snurfer Jake Burton began to develop the snowboard into the model we recognize today, with bindings that hold the user's boots firmly in place on the board. This allowed snowboarders to perform jumps and trick moves while keeping the board under their control.

▶ A snowboarder jumps in the air to perform a trick on a half pipe.

PIPE DREAMS

In 1992, Doug Waugh invented the Pipe Dragon. Built from farm machinery, it cut out and smoothed giant u-shaped channels in snow, known as half-pipes, for snowboarders to perform tricks in.

Early snowboards were made of laminated wood, just like ten-pin bowling lanes.

71

49

Vid o games

The first computer games were devised at universities. For instance, a version of noughts and crosses called *OXO* was developed in Cambridge, UK, by A.S. Douglas in 1952. A decade later, Steve Russell at MIT (Massachusetts Institute of Technology) produced the first computer action game, *Spacewar!* Two players used keyboards to control battling spaceships.

GAMES AT HOME

Ralph H. Baer invented the first console that could be plugged into a TV in 1968, which went on sale in 1972 as the Magnavox Odyssey. In 1976, the Fairchild Channel F became the first home machine to use games stored on separate cartridges, followed the next year by the first full-colour cartridge games machine, the Atari 2600. With games such as *PacMan* and *Space Invaders*, the Atari 2600 was a huge hit.

ARCADE ACTION

Computer games were first made accessible to the public in arcades. *Computer Space* (a 1971 version of *Spacewar!*) produced by Nolan Bushnell and Ted Dabney was the first mass-produced arcade computer game. The pair would also create the Atari 2600. In 1978, *Space Invaders* was released. Invented by Tomohiro Nishikado, it became one of the most popular games of all time.

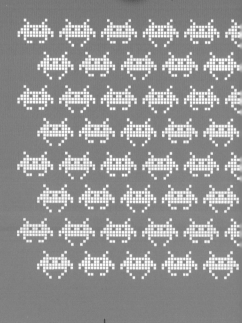

HANDHELD GAMES

The first handheld games machine was the Microvision, designed by Jay Smith in 1979. It was followed by the Atari Lynx in 1987 – the first handheld console with a colour screen. Next came the Game Boy, created by Gunpei Yokoi, of the Japanese games giant Nintendo in 1989. It became the world's most popular handheld gamer, selling more than 118 million units.

▲ A child raises her arm to move her character's arm in a motion-tracking game.

MOTION SENSING

Kinect for Xbox went on sale in 2010. It was the first popular games device to dispense with controllers such as joysticks. Instead, cameras and sensors in the device track players' movements and convert them into in-game instructions.

◀ The Game Boy used removable cartridges that allowed users to play different games.

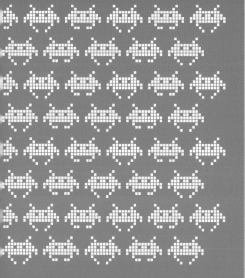

▲ Space invaders *was the first shooter game to feature an enemy that shot back, and the first to feature a high score.*

GAMES HALL OF FAME

ALEXEY PAJITNOV

The Russian invented the falling blocks puzzle, *Tetris*, in 1985. It is now the world's most downloaded paid game with more than 500 million copies on smartphones alone.

MARKUS PERSSON

Most modern games are produced by teams of designers, but the Swede, Markus Persson, created the open-world block game *Minecraft* on his own in 2009. It has since sold more than 70 million copies.

SHIGERU MIYAMOTO

Shigeru Miyamoto produced the platform game *Donkey Kong*, for Nintendo in 1981, and later invented the world's best-selling action games series *Mario* (509 million units sold so far).

Inventing the future

In the future, inventors will continue to astound, amaze and amuse us with their ideas. Some future inventions may tackle ecological problems, while others could improve people's day-to-day lives or enable us to live longer and more healthily.

NANOTECHNOLOGY

Nanotechnology involves building incredibly small devices that can only be measured in nanometres. A nanometre is a one thousand millionth of a metre – a single sheet of paper is around 100,000 nanometres thick. Constructing machines at this tiny scale could lead to far faster computers, self-repairing materials and many other advances.

▲ *Nanotechnology may allow us to create tiny machines that could attack viruses directly inside the body.*

EVERYDAY INNOVATIONS

Some inventions currently being developed may have an impact on your future life.

▶ *One of Google's self-driving cars.*

MIND CONTROL

Future electronic gadgets may be controlled by your thoughts alone, using headsets containing transmitters that connect with your brain. Artificial arms have already been invented that can be controlled by a person's thoughts.

DRIVERLESS VEHICLES

Cars equipped with sensors and navigation aids can drive themselves, ferrying people from place to place in the future. Companies like Google, Audi, Ford and Toyota are working on cars that can drive and navigate themselves some or all of the time.

In 2014, a nanomotor was built that was so small it could fit inside a single human cell.

74

NANOBOTS

Future inventions in nanotechnology may lead to incredibly small nano-robots or 'nanobots'. These might be able to repair materials, clean up pollution or even work on the human body from the inside, repairing tissue without surgery, fighting disease or scrubbing blood vessels free of the fatty deposits which can cause heart disease.

NANOPARTICLES

These are tiny particles (less than 100 nanometres in size) with certain properties which can be added to larger particles of a different material to change how it behaves. Nanoparticles are already being used in some substances to make them stronger or more stain resistant. Zinc dioxide nanoparticles, for example, are added to some sunscreens to help block out harmful UV rays from the Sun.

▲ Titanium dioxide nanotubes, each 10,000 smaller than the width of a human hair.

-3D- PRINTING

3D printers lay down a thin layer of metal, plastic or some other material again and again to build up a three-dimensional object from a digital file stored in its memory. Chuck Hull is considered the father of 3D printing, having invented the first 3D printers during the 1980s. 3D printers are already at work in industries, producing vehicle parts, as well as toys and medical items, such as dental crowns, false teeth and other artificial body parts.

▶ In 2014, parts of the Swedish supercar, Koenigsegg One:1, were produced using a 3D printer.

FULLY FLEXIBLE SCREENS

Computing screens are being developed from lightweight flexible films that may one day see you able to fold, or roll up, a computer tablet like you would a sheet of paper.

BATTERIES

Inventors are developing lighter, smaller batteries that hold a higher charge, so that electronic gadgets can be built lighter and last longer without the need for recharging.

◀ A 3D printer creating a three-dimentional plastic object, layer by layer.

WHO'S WHO?
Great inventors

Curiosity about the world and a desire to improve people's lives have been driving people to become inventors for thousands of years. Many of the earliest advances were made by unknown innovators in the ancient civilizations of Egypt, China, India, Rome and Greece. Here are some of the world's greatest inventors.

Archimedes
(287 BCE–212 BCE)

This Greek scientist invented a screw pump for drawing water from rivers and developed pulley systems that could lift giant loads.

Leonardo da Vinci
(1452–1519)

The great Italian artist came up with many inventions that were way ahead of their time including flying machines and armoured cars.

Benjamin Franklin
(1706–1790)

This US statesman and writer invented lightning rods, a new type of wood-burning stove and bifocal spectacles.

Eli Whitney
(1765–1825)

Whitney's system of interchangeable standard parts for guns pioneered mass-production techniques in the United States.

John Boyd Dunlop
(1840–1921)

This Scotsman invented the first practical pneumatic (air-filled) rubber tyres, which gave a more comfortable ride than solid tyres.

Thomas Edison
(1847–1931)

This prolific American scientist invented the phonograph and improved telephones, light bulbs and electricity generation.

George Washington Carver (c.1860–1943)

The pioneering African-American scientist invented dyes, paper, adhesives and many other products derived from peanuts.

Katharine Burr Blodgett (1898–1979)

An American chemist, Blodgett invented non-reflective glass that was widely used for film projectors, cameras and submarine periscopes.

Sergei Korolev (1907–1966)

A Russian engineer who developed the first artificial satellite in space and was head of the team that launched the first man into space.

Grace Murray Hopper (1906-1992)

A US Navy officer, Hopper pioneered computer languages and invented the first compiler that translated written language into computer code.

Otis Boykin (1920–1982)

The American was the inventor of many electronic components, including precision resistors and a control unit for heart pacemakers.

Stephanie Kwolek (1923-2014)

This US materials scientist developed a number of synthetic plastics including Kevlar, which is used in protective clothing.

Tim Berners-Lee (born 1955)

British inventor Tim Berners-Lee, the son of computer scientists, invented the World Wide Web, produced the first website and developed HTML.

Ajay Bhatt (born 1957)

This Indian computer engineer is the co-inventor of the universal serial bus (USB), which allows computers and other devices to communicate.

GLOSSARY

ALLOY
A metal made up of two (or more) different kinds of metal.

ANTISEPTIC
A substance that cleans and sterilizes, preventing the spread of infection.

CATHODE RAY TUBE
A type of vacuum tube in which images are produced by electrons striking a special light-emitting screen.

CELLULOID
A type of plastic made from plant fibres and used to make movie film in the early 20th century.

EMBOSSING
A method of raising something, such as a letter, slightly above a flat surface.

EXHAUST
Waste gases expelled from a vehicle or machine during operation.

FILAMENT
A fine wire through which an electric current can be passed.

FORCE
Something that affects the motion and movement of an object.

GRAVITY
A force which draws objects to one another and causes things to fall to Earth.

HTML
Hyper Text Markup Language – the computer code used to create webpages.

HTTP
Hypertext Transfer Protocol – a set of rules for transferring data across the World Wide Web using clickable links called hyperlinks.

INCANDESCENT
Emitting light when heated.

INNOVATIVE
To be new, original or advanced, usually improving on an existing concept.

INTERNAL COMBUSTION ENGINE
An engine that burns fuel (usually some form of oil) to generate power.

LASER
A device for producing an intense beam of single-coloured light.

LENS
A curved piece of glass used for focusing light rays and magnifying images.

LOCOMOTIVE
A powered railway vehicle that pulls other un-powered railway vehicles.

MACHINE
A device that performs a particular task (or tasks).

MASS PRODUCTION
The manufacture of large quantities of identical goods.

MICROPHONE
A device that converts sound into electrical signals, which can be amplified, recorded or transmitted.

MICROPROCESSOR
A complete processing system for a computer contained on a single chip.

PATENT
An official government document giving an inventor the exclusive rights to their invention.

PISTON
A cylinder or disc that moves up and down inside another cylinder as part of a machine.

PROPELLER
A device consisting of angled blades stretching out from a central point, which move a vehicle (such as a boat or a plane) when turned.

PROTOTYPE
A model of an invention or innovation, built to test it.

PULLEY
A wheel over which a rope or chain can be hung to redirect or reduce the force needed to lift a load.

RADIO WAVES
A form of invisible electromagnetism which can be used to carry information through the air.

REFLECTOR
A type of telescope that uses mirrors to gather and focus light.

REFRACTOR
A type of telescope that uses glass lenses to gather and focus light.

STEAM ENGINE
An engine that generates power via the heat energy of pressurized steam.

SYNTHETIC
Something that is artificial or human-made, rather than natural.

TELEGRAPH
A system for transmitting messages over long distances in the form of electrical signals – usually along a wire.

THRUST
A force that pushes in one direction.

TRANSISTOR
A device that can regulate, switch or amplify an electric current.

VACUUM TUBES
A glass tube from which nearly all the air has been removed, allowing an electric current to pass through it easily.

INDEX

3D printing 63, 75

aircraft 7, 14–17
antiseptics 60
artificial body parts 61

Bakelite 50
ballpoint pens 23, 29
Barbies 63
barcodes 4
batteries 44, 46, 75
Berners-Lee, Tim 43, 77
Bhatt, Ajay 77
bicycles 6, 8
Braille 32, 35

cameras 63
celluloid 50
central heating 22, 24
cinema 62, 64–5
compact discs (CDs) 67
computers 33, 40–1
    games 72–3
    mouse 5
CT scanners 58

dishwashers 22
diving equipment 7
driverless vehicles 74
dynamite 44, 47
Dyson, James 4

Edison, Thomas 5, 30, 39, 65, 66, 76
electromagnets 48
email 42
endoscopes 59
Engelbart, Douglas 5, 77

film 62, 64–5
frozen food 22, 26

hot-air balloons 6, 9
hypocausts 24

internal combustion engines 11
International Space Station 21, 25
Internet 33, 42

jet engines 7, 16–17

Kevlar 51

lasers 44, 53, 67
lenses 56
levers 44, 45
light bulbs 5, 23, 30

microscopes 56
microwave ovens 5, 22, 27

mobile phones 39
Morse Code 36
motor cars 12–13
MP3 67
MRI scanners 59

nanotechnology 63, 74–5
nylon 51

pacemakers 60
paper 33
phonographs 66
photography 63
plasters, sticking 61
plastics 50–1
printing press 32, 34
programming languages 41
prototypes 4
pulleys 44, 45

radiators 24
radio 32, 37
records 66
remote controllers 69
robots 45, 54–5, 75
rockets 19

safety pins 31
Sat Nav 20
satellites 20

smartphones 39
snowboards 71
space telescopes 57
spacecraft 7, 19–21
steam engines 6, 10
steam turbines 49
Styrofoam 51
submarines 7, 18

Teflon 51
telegraph 32, 36
telephones 33, 38–9
telescopes 45, 57
television 62, 68–9
tin openers 4
toasters 23
toilets, flushing 22, 25
trampolines 62, 70
transistors 44, 52

vacuum cleaners 4, 23, 28
Velcro 23, 31
video games 63, 72–3

wheels 6, 44
World Wide Web 33, 43
writing 32–3

X-rays 45, 58–9

zips 31

Picture credits (t=top, b=bottom, l=left, r=right, c=centre, fc=front cover, bc=back cover)

All images public domain unless otherwise indicated:
Alamy.com: 26tl Granger, NYC, 61br epa european pressphoto agency b.v., 63br B Christopher. *Dreamstime*: fc line 1 cr, line 2 cr, line 3 cl, line 4 c, line 5 cr, line 6 cl, c, r, line 7 l, bc t, b, line 1 cl, cr, r, line 2 l, cl, cr, 4bl, 4b, 4br, 5t, 5br, 6c, 7c, 7b, 8cl, 1bl, 12cl, 12bl, 12br, 13tr, 13cr, 13bl, 13br, 15cr, 16br, 17bl, 17bc, 17br, 19tl, 20bl, 22cr, 23tl, 23cr, 23b, 24c, 25tr, 25cl, 26cr, 26bl, 29br, 30tr, 30br, 31l, 31cl, 32c, 33tl,34tl,34tr, 34br, 36cr, 40b, 41tl, 43tl, 43b, 44bl, 44–45, 47c, 48, 49cr, 51cl, 51br, 52tr, 52bl, 53cl, 53bl, 56bl, 57tr, 58tr, 58b, 58br, 59tr, 59c, 60bl, 61tl, 62–63, 63bl, 65bl, 65br, 65tr, 67tr, 69cr, 70c, 70cr, 71b, 71tr, 72bl, 73cl, 73tr, 74t, 75bl, 75br, 76tc, 77bc. *Getty Images*: 28cr Science & Society Picture Library. *iStock.com*: fc line 1 l, cl, line 2 l, cl, c, r, line 3 l, r, line 5 l, cl, cr, line 6 l, line 7 cl, r, bc line 1 l, c, line 2 r, 8ct, 8tr, 8b, 9c, 27br, 46cl, 46bl, 54–55tl, 55br. *Shutterstock.com*: 65tl, 75–76.
Wikimedia Commons: fc line 1r DaimlerChrysler AG, fc line 7cr Graferocommons, bc line 2cr William Warby, 4cl Royal Society, 5bl SRI International, 10cl Tony Hisgett, 10bl PTG Dudva, 16bl Ralf Manteufel, 17t Gryffindor, 17cr Adrian Pingstone, 19br AElfwine, 28bl F. Duten, 35bl Nbanerjee, 36cl Geni, 37cl Cardiff Council Flat Holm Project, 38c Zubro, 39bc Redrum0486, 40tr Carsten Ullrich, 40cl Dksen, 41br Oo1326, 42tl Steve Jurvetson, 45tr Eric Gaba, 46tr GuidoB, 41cl Sam Lionheart, 50cl Bart, 50br William Warby, 51tl Erik Liljeroth, Nordic Museum, Sweden, 56tr Wellcome Trust, 59br Benutzer:Kalumet, 60–61b Wellcome Trust, 61cr Wellcome Trust, 63tr NotFromUtrecht, 65cr Victorgrigas, 66t Musik- och teatermuseet, 66br Mediatus, 68tr Holger.Ellgaard, 69tr Denelson83, 69c Jim Rees, 70br Tim Blake, 73c Official GDC, 73bc ImagineCup, 73br Sklathill, 74br Michael Shick, 75c Argonne National Laboratory, 75cr Navigator84, 77cr Alex Handy, 77bl Chemical Heritage Foundation, 77br Intel Free Press.